ÀJÍKẸ́ ỌMỌLỌLÁ

OVERCOMING LIFE'S TRAVAILS

Rise Above Life's Travails and Embrace
the Extraordinary Within You

Author's Contact
Email: overcominglifestravails@gmail.com

Published by Lodeta Media & Publishing
A division of Lodeta Consulting LLC
www.lodetaconsulting.com

Dedication

To my late father, Lawyer Aseph Olayemi ABOGUN talias TOUGHITY I know you are smiling down on your daughter now. Thank you for your undying love that always inspires me to gofor it.

To my dear mother, Roseline Oluwagbemiga ABOGUN. Thank you for all the love, nurture, and discipline you never compromised over me. I am eternally grateful to you Mummy.

To Lesley Oyinkansola YOPA and Darren Adeife YOPA, my niece and nephew of inestimable measure. You know Aunty Lola will bend repeatedly for you to reach your God-given destinies. I love you both very greatly! May The Good Lord who has begun a good work in you bring it to completion till the day of Christ.

To everyone suffering wrongfully, may God Almighty intervene quickly in your situation.

What People are Saying About The Book

"Overcoming Life's Travail" is a powerful and inspiring book that challenges us to redefine our relationship with adversity. It empowers readers to overcome life's challenges and tap into their full potential with every practical principles outlined therein

The author's candid storytelling and insightful advice make this book a true gem for those in search of guidance on their journey to destiny.I highly recommend this book to anyone ready to embark on a transformative journey toward a life of purpose, success, and fulfillment. It is a beacon of hope and a source of wisdom that should be on every bookshelf.

Adeola Atekoja. Author & Lead Consultant Lodeta Media & Publishing, Baltimore, Maryland.USA

I have known Minister Ajike Omolola for more than a decade now. She is a motivator, impacting people's lives and making them understand that they can live more fulfilled lives when they have faith in God and believe in God's potential deposited in them.

The message in this book: *Overcoming Life's Travail* is a must for anyone wanting to live an overcomer's life and end up a champion.

John 16:33 encourages us to be at peace because Jesus has overcome the world for us.

You will be tremendously blessed as you study her teachings and allow your faith to increase.

Moses Amubioya, True worshipers Ministries,1 Antoine Burdell, 93600 Alnay Sous Bois France

Using a blend of historical, biblical, and philosophical lenses, the author has delivered a literary masterpiece relevant to all ages that is contemporary and challenging, and almost prophetic in dimensions. The book is a conscientious trip through life that brings the reality of daily living to our senses. It resonates to self-building beliefs that can help one overcome the travails of life and be successful indeed.

"The difference between the great and successful .... and the mediocre and poor .... is their disposition to the circumstances of life,"She writes, and rightly so.

This work is an inspiration, a life roadmap and should be the envy of motivational speakers, and a companion to people in adversity and for all seasons.

-Pastor F.O. C. Odili, President, Synergic Impact Incorporated, London, UK.

This is a great book that everyone should take advantage of. God did not promise us life without troubles and challenges but in every travail of life, there's always a way of escape one is free from challenges and if we must be successful, we must learn how to overcome life'stroubles.

Challenges are proof that God's presence is still with you. At the peak of every success, testimony and breakthrough, the trials are intensified. What we go through often is pointer to the problem God want us to solve.

I recommend this book **"Overcoming Life's Travails"** by Ajike Omolola.

By the wealth of the contents of this profound book, I know someone will rise above their limitations and become a success. Grab this book, eat it, and manifest the success you desire. You Will Rise Again!

-Bishop Dr. Alabi Oluwaseyi, Lead Pastor, Breakthrough Covenant Christian Church Lagos, Nigeria.

I have known Lola for well over twenty years. We use tofondly call her AJ back in our secondary school days andI have seen her genuineness with undying, unending, and unbroken commitment to the things of God and His kingdom. Back then, many of the brothers within the Christian fold we all belonged to looked forward to having her as their future bride because they all believed she was going to be a great "ministry material" as we fondly say.

Anyway, over the years of knowing her as a sister full of grace, I have seen her go through stuff in life that an ordinary person would have been completely broken by and would never rise again; but seeing her bounce back many times isproof that she has been thoroughly groomed by the word of God as I have always seen her to be.

Now, this book: *Overcoming Life's Travails,* is a narrative of the manifestation of a tested and proven life of Lola. Her struggles are oddly, inexplicable tough times with a rising to victory and triumph over numerous challenges in her quest to fulfill God's purpose for her life.

After going through this volume, I'm confident and proud to recommend this book to as many who want to and are really looking forward to seeing the triumph of faith and the victory of the knowledge of God's word in their journey to fulfilling destiny. This is a masterpiece that is handed down to a generation that needs a revival and restoration of hope, faith, and finding purpose in life.

Please, go through it with an open heart and be ready to navigate through the journey of your life with every necessary material you can find in every chapter of this book which will take you through every phase of change you will encounter in your journey to destiny. See you at the top!

-Emmanuel Bamidele Okusanya (PEBO), Lead Pastor of RCCG EKKLESIA HOUSE, McKinney Texas, USA.

Oh wow! What a great and insightful book. It brought to bear the travails of life and how to conquer come what it may. The book is simple, self-explanatory, and profound. I didn't want to stop reading. I can't wait for more. Blessings!

-Yinka Jenrola, Director, EJN VenturesLagos, Nigeria

Foreword

There are inevitable absolutes in life. One of such is trouble. Trouble is normal, at every stage in our growth process. As obviously attested by the author, Ajike Omolola, "It doesn't matter who we are or where we are from, we would encounter one or more challenges and difficulties on our way to destiny. No one is immune from the troubles of life".

Our Sovereign Lord, Jesus Christ affirms that in this life, we shall have trials andtribulations, but we must be of good cheer because He has overcome the world. He also promised that He will never leave us, nor forsake us. This resonates as a direct response to the emphatic prayer of the Psalmist, "May the Lord answer you in the day of trouble".

Very remarkably, our human responses to trajectories of life vary. In the words of the writer, "Most people give up on their life's journey when they encounter obstacles and thorns on their path. Others abandon their dreams, ambitions, and pursuit of purpose and live as victims of circumstances for the rest of their lives. Yet, a few are able to overcome the travails of life and walk into their glorious destiny to fulfill life's purpose and accomplish their dreams".

As the Master of life Himself has established victory for us, leveraging on Hispathways, so is the assurance for success against the vicissitudes of life, knowing fullythere is an enabling grace to excel.

This work narrated the writer and other notable profiles' struggles and how they honed divine principles to overcome challenges. It thus serves as a compendium for embracing the extraordinary strength within us to rise above life's travails.

I recommend this masterpiece, *Overcoming Life's Travails*, by my daughter in our common faith, to everyone who desires to win in life by righteousness; for those who embrace the lifestyle of maintaining contact in a fallen world, without contamination as part of the indomitable new breed **and** without greed in the areas of life they find themselves in.

Remember, you were born for more than the average life; you were born for greatness and a life of purpose and impact. Go andexcel.

-Pastor Tunde Bakare, Serving Overseer, The Citadel Global Community Church (CGCC), Lagos, Nigeria.

Acknowledgment

I t's a great privilege to have the breath of life and all thanks to God Almighty for surrounding me with wonderful people.

Firstly, I would love to thank my dad in the Faith, Dr. Tunde Bakare the Serving Overseer of the Citadel Global Community Church, Lagos, Nigeria for all the love and always holding me up before God. I am very grateful Sir. Your teachings are life changing.

To your darling wife Mrs. Bamidele Bakare, the Authentic Mrs. B! Thank you, Ma, for your consistent love and support. Your presence in my life is a huge encouragement to keep going. And also to the entire leadership of the Citadel Global Community Church, Lagos, Nigeria.

Chief Andrew Iduh, President, Nigerians in Diaspora Organization (NIDO), Spain Chapter. You are a father with a difference. Thank you, sir, for always looking out for me and standing by me all the way. You are indeed a great man with a good large heart.

Mr. and Mrs. Chike Maduegbuna, Mr. and Mrs. Idy Enang, Mrs. Honor Onyebuchukwu, and Mr. Benzak Uzuegbu I want to thank you for your unrelenting support.

To my church leaders in France: Pastor Marc Rizzolio, Pastor Innocent Essone – Ntoutoumou, Pastor Ange-Laurent Coddy, Pastor Christophe Boulevard, Pastor Samuel Buot, Pastor Eduardo Haddad of the Eglise Unisson. Thank you all for relentlessly feeding me with the Word of God.

My appreciation also goes to Mr. & Mrs. Babatunde Lawal, Mr. & Mrs. Oluwayemi Ajimisan and Mr. & Mrs. Olusegun Adejobi of Yoruba Descendants Association in France (YODAFRANCE). Thank you for making France more conducive for me.

Mrs. Irene Guei, Mrs. Henriette Mendy and Mrs. Abimbola Onwuchekwa, for being wonderful mothers to me. Thank you for all your counsel and prayers.

My appreciation also goes to my Equinoxe Family. To Mr. Osaretin David, my Spanish cameraman.

I would love to acknowledge my best friends Mr and Mrs Felix Ogbe.

I would also like to acknowledge my Camera crew in France. In the persons of Mr Obaloluwaseyi Akinbobola and Mr Feyisayo Rufus (MC Jagal).

My gratitude also goes to all members of Fight the Good Fight of Faith with Lola family.

Lastly, my dear Coach and Sister Mrs. Adeola Atekoja, CEO, Lodeta Consulting LLC, and my Editor Dr. Clement Ogedegbe, and the rest of the publishing team, for your staunch support in making this project a reality.

Thank you and God bless you all. Shalom!

Contents

Introduction

From the time of *the fall of man,* our world became a world of troubles, sorrow, and pain. We are born into such a world of adversity howbeit, with a purpose, mission and calling and as we journey towards our destiny, we encounter obstacles, hurdles, and bottlenecks. From childhood to adulthood, we are exposed to life's travails and ugly circumstances, many of which we have no control over. These circumstances come in various forms ranging from sicknesses, diseases, poverty, homelessness, delayed marriages, rape, divorce, barrenness, abuse, loss of loved ones, and failure in business, academics, or political pursuit. It doesn't matter who we are or where we are from, we would encounter one or more challenges and difficulties on our way to destiny. No one is immune from the troubles of life.

While it is true that we all face troubles and travails on our way to destiny, we all, however, do not react to them in the same way. Most people give up on their life's journey when they encounter obstacles and thorns on their path. Others abandon their dreams, ambitions, and pursuit of purpose and live as victims of circumstances for the rest of their lives. Yet, a few people are able to overcome the travails of life and walk into their glorious destiny to fulfil their life's purpose and accomplish their dreams. This is the reason there are only very few great and successful people in our world today and a multitude of mediocre people living a mundane life.

Often times, when we see great and successful people, we are tempted to believe that their life's journey is void of challenges and that life is very kind to them. We erroneously conclude that they are succeeding and fulfilling their purpose because they walked a seamless path to get to their destiny. What we fail to realize is that no one has a completely smooth path to destiny; we all encounter problems, hurdles, and difficulties on the way to fulfilling our destiny. It is our reaction to these challenges that determine whether we would be successful and reach our place of purpose or if we would quit and live the rest of our lives in mediocrity.

To therefore, become successful and walk in our life's purpose, we must learn how to overcome the travails of life that buffet us and try to prevent us from reaching our destiny. This is the reason I have written this book; to help you rise above the travails of life and embrace the extraordinary within you. You were born for more than the average life; you were born for greatness and a life of purpose and impact.

Throughout my life's journey, I encountered troubles, travails, pain, sorrows, and ugly circumstances that would have truncated my destiny and prevented me from reaching my place of purpose. I, however, was able to navigate through them to reach my promised land-the place of purpose, impact, and fulfilled dreams. I have shared in this book my story and those of other great and successful people who overcame the troubles of life to fulfil their unique purpose and dreams. The principles and secrets we applied have been outlined here for you and anyone else who wants to win and overcome the travails of their lives.

There is no need to continue to live in self-pity as a victim of circumstances and there is no point living in mediocrity when you can live an extraordinary life. The solution is right here in your hands. I do hope that you will learn from the stories in this book, apply the principles therein and walk into your glorious destiny.

See you at the top! Cheers!

Chapter One
THE JOURNEY OF LIFE

A fetus is formed in the womb of a woman and receives nourishment, immunity, and warmth from its mother and has no worries about anything, neither does it understand what life outside the uterus is like. After nine months, that fetus is born as a baby and introduced into our world; a world he neither knows anything about nor does he know the purpose for which he was sent there. So he starts a journey of life with zero knowledge of where he is heading and how he would get there. The story is the same for every human who has ever **set** foot in this earthly realm. We all come here knowing nothing about **this world** and what would happen to us as we journey through life. Many people have wondered and asked what life we is about and why are born into this world. In the same vein, many answers have been given as to why we exist and are born into this world. Whatever the answers are, one thing is certain and that is we all would journey through life in a bid to reach our destinations-the purpose of our being. Just as our faces are different, so are our paths to our destinations.

Everyone Has a Path

There is no arguing that God does nothing unless there is a purpose for it. He creates nothing if He has no purpose for it. This means that our birth and life are for a purpose. You were born for a purpose; I was born for a purpose, and we would not be in existence today had God not sent us here to fulfill specific purposes. That is why when you look at the world today, you would see doctors, engineers, lawyers, teachers, pastors, ministers, social activists, leadership coaches and motivational speakers. A myriad of occupations! They are all doing what they feel they were born to do to make the world a better place and they are fulfilling their life's purpose. While we all grow from the little baby that was born knowing nothing to become an adult with a passion and desire to follow what we perceive to be the purpose of our lives, our paths to achieving our purpose would be different and so would be our life's experiences. From birth to adulthood to death, we would have different experiences and follow different paths. Some people's path to destiny would be a bit smooth while others would be rough, some would walk on thorns while others would walk on roses, some would reach their destination faster while others would arrive later; we all have different paths and different destinations. The journey of life is not the same for everyone and each one of us must brace up for whatever our lotin life may be. In his award-winning novel, *A Winter Dream,* Richard Paul Evans speaks through one of his characters about adversity:

"My Dear Son,

I am so very proud of you. Now, as you embark on a new journey, I'd like to share this one piece of advice. Always, always remember that - adversity is not a detour. It is part of the path."

Unlike in our mother's womb, where we have no worries and get everything we need, our life's journey after we are born is not a walk in the park. Life is full of ups and downs, good times and bad times, suffering, hardship, pain and sorrows, sicknesses, diseases, deaths, and unforeseen circumstances. Many are crushed by the travails and troubles of life; some others abandon their dreams and life's pursuit in the face of challenging situations and yet there are those who fight with a never-give-up spirit to overcome all the challenges and troubles that life throws at them until they reach their desired destination and fulfil their life's purpose. The latter group is those who, despite the thorns on their path, walk through, enduring the pain and sufferings of life to get to their promised land-their place of purpose and impact. These people who fight through adversity have come to terms with a life that is full of suffering, pain, and hardship and understand how to seize opportunities to pick themselves up from the ashes and overcome the bottlenecks on our path to destiny.

"Although the world is full of suffering, it is also full of overcoming it," said Hellen Keller, blind and deaf speaker, teacher, and motivator. She is a class act of overcoming adversity.

Most people give up in the face of challenges and abandon their life's pursuit because they are never prepared for challenges and the ugly circumstances of life. They don't have the slightest idea that life could be cruel sometimes and they had hoped that their life's journey would be seamless. Why is this the case? It is probably because as infants, nothing prepares us for the challenges of life. We are loved by parents and relatives, kissed, cuddled, given whatever we want and pampered. We do not worry about unemployment for we have no idea what it means. We are not bothered about where the next meal would come from as our mother's breasts are readily available to supply us milk when we need itand we care not about inflation, economic recession, childlessness, delayed marriages, or divorce because we have no idea that such things exist. All we know at such a young age is love and care, eating and sleeping. We know nothing about the travails of life, the cruelty of life's circumstances and hence think that life is a bed of roses.

Life is Not a Bed of Roses

I, just like many infants, grew up enjoying the love and care of my parents and relatives and having no care in the world. I was born into a unique family and was my father's favorite as he would shower love and care on me and hold me close to his side whenever he was home. Being the child of a Father who was a Lawyer, I was introduced early to reading as I would watch and mimic my dad whenever he was reading. My parents called me *Professor* because I learned how to read early, and they felt there was no need for me to attend nursery school. When I eventually started primary school, I became the beloved of my teachers as I was a very brilliant child. I always took the second or third position in my exams. I soon joined the soccer team and played as a striker. Although I never thought I was a good footballer, I always had a lot of praise and commendations for playing a good game at the end of every match. Being a vibrant and brilliant student and loved by other students and teachers, I eventually became a school prefect before I was done with primary school. All through primary school, my parents provided everything I needed; notebooks, textbooks, uniforms, pens, clothes, shoes, toys, school fees, food, and everything else that I needed as a child. I didn't have to worry about anything as life and everyone around me was good to me. I thus concluded in my mind as a child that life would always be kind and fair to me and that I would have everything I need and walk a seamless path to my destiny: the purpose of my existence, my ambitions, and my dreams.

I, just like most people, thought that life was a bed of roses and that it would always be void of challenges, travails, and adversity. Nothing prepared me for the adversities of life as no one told me that life is not a bed of roses. It took painful experiences and bitter encounters with the cruel hands of life to learn and understand that the road to destiny is full of thorns and that if I must succeed in the pursuit of my dreams, ambitions, and life's purpose, I must walk a rough path to get there.

"Nobody is exempt from the trials of life, but everyone can always find something positive in everything even in the worst of times."
— Roy T. Bennett, **author of the Life of Heart**

Just like I used to, most people today still think that life is a bed of roses and that all they need is to just have a dream, an ambition, and a purpose and that "lines would fall in pleasant places" for them as they take a stroll to their destiny. Some other people erroneously think that because they are Christians and love the Lord, they would be immune to the challenges of life. There are also others who think because they were born into a wealthy family, life would always smile at them. Yet another mindset defines living abroad and having British, American or Canadian citizenship as a shield from the agony of life. What a delusion! Life is not a respecter of persons; adversity finds us all, no matter our faith, financial background, citizenship, or country of residence. Life has a fair share of troubles for every human living on this earth. Even the Bible teaches that human beings have a short time to live and that our lives are full of trouble:

Man, that is born of a woman is of few days and full of troubles
(Job 14:1 KJV)

Unless we realize this truth and come to terms with it, we will have a hard time managing the challenges and travails of life that hit us on our path to destiny. We must realize that in life, we would encounter tough times, difficult situations, and unpalatable happenings some of which would almost crush us, demoralize us, and make us want to abandon our life's pursuits. To win in life and conquer the travails of life, we must first accept the fact that we live in a world of challenges and troubles and that sooner or later we will encounter them. By accepting the fact that troubles and difficult times are part of life, we do not run away when life pours its venom on us; we stand and fight to overcome whatever it is that is standing in our way of reaching our destiny and fulfilling our dreams.

The difference between the great and successful people in our society and the mediocre and poor people is their disposition to the circumstances of life. The difference between those who achieve their dreams and ambitions and those who give up on the way to destiny is that the former **can** brace themselves up for the challenges of life while the latter bend and surrender to them. The former understand that the troubles of life are stepping stones to greatness and a life of impact while the latter see them as limitations and hence shy away from them.

26

"Beautiful souls are shaped by ugly experiences." — Mashona Dhliwayo, Canadian based Philosopher, Entrepreneur, and author

No one truly becomes great who does not first overcome challenges and difficulties. Greatness is born in the place of pain and travail. The scriptures say:

Before she travailed, she brought forth.
before her pain came, she was delivered of a man-child.
Who hath heard such a thing?
who hath seen such things?
Shall the earth be made to bring forth in one day?
or shall a nation be born at once?
for as soon as Zion travailed, she brought forth her children.
(Isaiah 66:7-8 AKJV)

From the verses above, we see that it was as soon as Zion travailed that she brought forth her children. It is in the place of travail that children are born. Children, in this scripture, could represent greatness, success, dreams, ambitions, business ideas, your life's purpose, and everything else you want to achieve. There is a nation inside of you, a calling and purpose over your life and unless you go through pain and difficulties, you would most likely never birth any of them. The troubles of life come to help you birth your greatness and prepare you for your destiny; so, instead of running away from them, brace yourself to overcome them. Ebinezar Gnanasekaran, counseling psychologist explains it this way:

"No one is born with success. God shapes trials, tribulations, and frustrations to make you succeed. It is always darkest before the dawn."

Life teaches us important lessons that we need to succeed when we arrive at our promised land, our place of impact and exploits, through the pains and sufferings we encounter on our way to getting there. We grow in skills, experience, knowledge, and wisdom through the things we suffer. Concerning Jesus Christ, the Bible says that he learned obedience through the things he suffered.

Though he were a son yet learned he obedience by the things which he suffered.
(Hebrews 5:8 KJV)

From the foregoing, it is easy to see that perseverance, determination, patience; courage, self-belief, and every virtue that is needed to succeed in life and become great are learned and cultivated in the place of adversity and difficulties. These are the very virtues that make the great, great, and the successful, successful.

You will encounter obstacles. You will make mistakes. Be grateful for both. Your obstacles and mistakes will be your greatest teachers. And the only way to not make mistakes in this life is to do nothing, which is the biggest mistake of all.
- Richard Paul Evans

Anyone who desires greatness and success in life must therefore embrace travails and difficulties and perish the idea that life is a bed of roses.

The man who runs away from challenges will never learn and he who dislikes troubles may as well forget about becoming great and successful. For it is through pain and difficulty that greatness and success are born. Throughout the pages of this book, you shall read about the stories of many great and successful people who through pain and difficulties fought their way to the top; from Ben Carson, to Nick Vujicic, to Hellen Keller, to Joyce Meyer, to Paula White, to Nelson Mandela, and a host of many other successfulpeople whose names history would never forget. I have also shared my personal experience with pain and difficulty and how I travailed and fought my way to reach my place of purpose and impact.

While most of us would not experience the challenges and troubles of life from childhood, there are those who, even from birth, would be welcomed into this world with pain and adversity. These are bedeviled with birth pangs and travail before they can even understand what life is about. Their fight to overcome the troubles of life begins at infanthood and we do not need a soothsayer to decipher that these are born for greatness; because as we already stated, through pain, adversity, and difficulties is greatness born.

One example that comes to mind easily when we talk about being born into a world of hardship, pain, and troubles and facing difficulties from infanthood is Nick Vujicic.

Nick Vujicic (Nicholas James Vujicic), is an internationally renowned Christian evangelist, author, and motivational speaker whose message of perseverance, determination, and zeal to overcome life's challenges has provided succor and inspiration to multitudes of people across the globe.

Nick was born in Melbourne, Australia on 4th December 1982 to Dusanka and Borislav Vujicic, Serbian immigrants from Yugoslavia. There was, however, something striking about his birth. He was born with a rare genetic syndrome called tetra-Amelia; a disorder in which a child is born without arms and legs. Can you imagine the pain and travail of living the rest of your life without arms and legs! That was how Nick found himself as a child and he would live the rest of his life with the limitation of not having limbs.

The early days were difficult. Throughout his childhood, Nick not only dealt with the typical challenges of school and adolescence, but he also struggled with depression and loneliness. Nick constantly wondered why he was so different from all the other kids. He questioned the purpose of life and wondered if he even had a purpose.

Thanks to the love and support of his family, however, he was able to overcome his limitations and the painful circumstance of his birth to live life to the fullest.

After accepting the fact that we live in a world of pain and troubles, Nick, as a teenager, soon discovered his life's passion and purpose; to inspire people through public speaking. At the age of 19, he had his first speaking engagement and has since then continued to share his story with others teaching them that while life is full of challenges, those who do not give up in the face of these challenges can overcome them and fulfill their destiny and purpose. Nick has faced many rejections and setbacks because of his condition and has refused to give up his passion and purpose. He has gone ahead to become one of the most popular motivational speakers in the world, using his personal story to inspire his audience.

Nick's message of determination and perseverance has resonated with people of all ages and races, and he has blessed the lives of many people around the world. He has shared his story with millions, sometimes in stadiums filled to capacity, speaking to a range of diverse groups such as students, teachers, young people, business professionals and church congregations of all sizes.

Today this dynamic evangelist has accomplished more than most people achieve in a lifetime. He's an author, musician, actor, and evangelist.

He has authored several bestselling books, including "Life without Limits" and "Unstoppable," and he continues to inspire people across the world to overcome their challenges and use the ugly circumstances surrounding their lives as stepping stones to greatness.[1]

Through his personal experience and story, Nick has proven to us that though we live in a world of adversity and travails, we can through perseverance, determination and hard work overcome the bottlenecks on our way to destiny and fulfil our life's purpose and calling.

As we bring this chapter to a close, I would like to remind you that pain and adversity are part of life and every one of us must at some point in our lives be faced with challenges that we never anticipated. Most of these challenges would be there to prepare us for the great-unknown future ahead of us. It is therefore wise to prepare for them before they come and develop a mindset that accepts that life is not a bed of roses. The road to greatness and the fulfilment of your purpose would not be an easy one. It won't be a walk in the park. If you however, do not quit, you will reach your destination and fulfil the purpose of your being.

Nuggets

- Our birth and life are for a purpose. You were born for a purpose; I was born for a purpose, and we would not be in existence today had God not sent us here to fulfil specific purposes.

- We all have different paths and different destinations. The journey of life is not the same for everyone and each one of us must brace up for whatever our lost in life may be.

- Unlike in our mother's womb where we have no worries and get all our needs provided, our life's journey after we are born is not a walk in the park. Life is full of ups and downs, good times and bad times, suffering, hardship, pain and pleasure, sicknesses, diseases, deaths, and unforeseen circumstances.

- Many people are crushed by the travails and troubles of life; some others abandon their dreams and life's pursuit in the face of challenging situations and yet there are those who fight with a never-give-up spirit to overcome all the challenges and troubles that life throws at them until they reach their desired destination and fulfill their life's purpose.

- Those who despite the thorns on their path,

walk it nevertheless enduring the pain and sufferings of life eventually get to their promised land-their place of purpose and impact.

- You must come to terms with a life full of suffering, pain and hardship that affords us opportunities to pick ourselves up from the ashes and overcome the bottlenecks on our path to destiny.

- Nothing prepared me for the adversities of life. I learnt quite early that life is not a bed of roses. It took painful experience and bitter encounters at the cruel hands of life to learn and understand that the road to destiny is full of thorns and that if I must succeed in the pursuit of my dreams, ambitions and life's purpose, I must walk a rough path to get there.

- Life is not a respecter of persons; it happens to all of us, no matter our faith, financial background, citizenship or country of residence. Life has a fair share of troubles for every human being living on the earth.

- To win in life and conquer the travails of life, we must first accept that we live in a world full of challenges and troubles and that sooner or later we will encounter them.

- By accepting troubles and difficult times as

part of life, we do not run away when life pours its venom on us; we stand and fight to overcome adversitystanding in our way to destiny and the fulfillment of our dreams.

- No one truly becomes great without overcoming challenges and difficulties. Greatness is born in the place of pain and travail.

- There is a nation inside of you, a calling and purpose over your life and unless you go through pain and difficulties, you may never birth any of them.

- The troubles of life come to help you birth your greatness and prepare you for your destiny; so, instead of running away from them, brace yourself to overcome them.

- Life teaches us important lessons that we need to learn before we arrive at our promised land and our place of impact and exploits through the pains and sufferings, we encounter on our way there.

The man who runs away from challenges will never learn and he who dislikes troubles may as well forget about becoming great and successful. For it is through pain and difficulty that greatness and success are born.

Chapter Two
BOTTLENECKS ON THE WAY TO DESTINY

As we walk towards our life's purpose and the fulfilment of our dreams, ambitions, and life goals, we must be reminded that we live in a world of difficulties and that we will be met with hurdles, setbacks and bottlenecks on the way. The greatest challenges of life are often encountered on our way to destiny. These challenges come as bottlenecks to try to convince us to give up and surrender our pursuits; they come to make us believe that we are not good enough and that we lack what it takes to achieve our dreams and fulfil our calling and purpose. It is at this point that most people abandon their dreams and surrender their purpose for a life of mediocrity. Only very few people can overcome these bottlenecks and continue their journey until they reach their desired destination. In this chapter, we shall discuss how to overcome the bottlenecks on our way to destiny.

Only the Strong Survive

In Darwin's theory of evolution, the idea of natural selection is mooted in what is called *survival of the fittest*. He said that organisms live in an ever-changing environment and that in times of adverse environmental conditions, only those organisms that can adapt and endure these harsh conditions would survive while the rest that are not able to adapt will die off. A simple definition for the survival of the fittest theory is that those organisms which can adapt to change are more likely to survive long-term, and this includes their offspring. There have been many arguments and disagreements over Darwin's theory. However, when we look at our world today, we cannot deny that there is an element of truth in Darwin's analysis. We see all around us changing environmental conditions, changes in national and international economics, inflation, increased poverty, sicknesses, and diseases. As these conditions change and adversity sets in, many people are not able to adapt and survive; some give up the pursuit of their ambitions, dreams, and purpose, and others die from depression, diseases, and sicknesses. Only those people who understand that life is full of adversity and are able to adapt to the crushing circumstances of life keep moving against all odds towards the realization of their dreams and purpose. The strong desire to succeed makes them adjust to become better fitted for the challenges of life that come their way. This is why the survival of the fittest means that only the people with a strong desire to succeed and the ability to change as conditions change will achieve success.

How does this apply to me, you may ask? Well, it applies to you in every way. Because you live in this world of adversity and life is going to try to crush you! You will encounter not-so-favorableconditionsthat you never envisaged, some of your dreams and ambitions will be threatened and your life's purpose will be tested by the trials of life. Unless you learn to adjust and adapt, you would most likely give up and settle for less. Have you ever experienced poverty, a failed marriage, a failed business idea, delayed university admission, a serious medical condition, infertility, childlessness, visa denial, truncated travel plans? These are all adverse conditions that could stand as bottlenecks on your way to actualizing your dreams and life's purpose. How should you react to these and other traumatizing challenges? Quit? Get discouraged and give up, or quickly adapt and move on with life in the direction of your dreams?

Most people quit when they meet the hurdles of life, and they allow the bottlenecks on their way to destiny truncate their dreams. That is why the world is made up of very few successful people and a multitude of mediocre people. It is because hurdles are seen by many people to mean the end of their life's pursuits; they do not have enough zeal and desire to adapt and keep chasing their dreams and life goals. The few others who do succeed, do so because they realize that life is a race of survival of the fittest and that only the strong survive. They understand that in the game of hurdles, you do not quit when a hurdle is in your way! You leap over it. Hurdles are not meant to stop us; they are meant to be scaled. With every hurdle you meet on your life's journey, your first instinct shouldn't be to quit. Jump over it! Multiple award-winning basketball superstar Michael Jordan spent his life scaling limitations and he understands it better:

Obstacles don't have to stop you. If you run into a wall, don't turn around and give up. Figure out how to climb it, go through it or work around it.
-Michael Jordan

To overcome obstacles, you need a lot of energy, massive determination, and great zeal. You have to be strong, determined and zealous to overcome the hurdles of life.

What hurdles are you currently facing in your life? I want you to look them in the face and say, "I am not quitting, I am jumping over you; I must get to my destination, I must actualize my dreams and fulfil my purpose!" That is how you overcome the bottlenecks of life and add your name to the list of those people who through determination, and a strong desire to succeed, conquer the adversities of life.History is replete with people who faced difficult bottlenecks and hurdles on their way to the top, nevertheless, they survived against all odds and reached their destination. Helen Keller is an example of how through determination, zeal, and a relentless spirit, people can overcome the hurdles of life.

On June 27, 1880, Helen Keller was born in Tuscumbia, Alabama, with her senses intact. It wasn't until she was 18 months old that she was stricken with a mysterious illness that robbed her of sight and sound.

While she found ways to communicate with her parents, Arthur H. Keller and Kate Adams Keller, as well as her friend and the child of Keller's cook,

Martha Washington, Helen was prone to outbursts when she was not understood.

The outbursts grew in frequency and, when Helen was six years old, she and her father paid a visit to a distinguished oculist in Baltimore, who had been successful in rectifying similar cases. While nothing could be done to restore Helen's sight, Arthur Keller was advised to consult Dr. Alexander Graham Bell. Helen and her father left immediately for Washington, D.C., in search of Bell. Helen admired Bell immediately. He understood her crude signs, and their initial interview would lead to friendship, companionship, and a love that would compel Helen to dedicate her eventual autobiography, The Story of my Life, to Bell.

Bell advised Arthur Keller to write to the director of the Perkins Institution for the Blind in Boston to inquire if they could recommend a qualified teacher to educate Helen. This communication resulted in what Helen considers, the most important day of her life. Anne Mansfield Sullivan arrived at the Keller household three months before Helen turned seven years old. Within six months of her arrival in Tuscumbia, Sullivan taught Helen hundreds of vocabulary words, using the manual alphabet, multiplication, and Braille.

In 1890, when Helen was nine years old, she learned of a deaf and blind girl in Norway who was taught how to speak. Determined to learn as well, Helen and Sullivan ventured to the Horace Mann School for the Deaf in Boston to consult the principal, Sarah Fuller. Fuller began instructing Helen at once. Passing Helen's hand lightly over her face, Fuller would let her feel the position of her tongue and lips when she made a sound. Helen then imitated every motion, and, in an hour, she had learned six elements of speech. On returning home, Sullivan tirelessly took over as Helen's speech instructor.

Sullivan eventually traveled with Helen to the Perkins School, where she began receiving a formal education, and even to Radcliffe College where Helen earned her degree. Sullivan was a loyal teacher and companion until the day she died in 1936.

Despite being blind and deaf, Helen Keller went on to become a world-famous speaker and author, an advocate for people with disabilities, and an active member of the socialist party. Many people with normal sight and hearing are not able to achieve anything of worth in their lifetime, but Helen overcame the hurdles of blindness and deafness to live a purpose-driven life and accomplish unimaginable feats. Below are some of her accomplishments:

-Helen learned to speak in 1890, at nine years old. This is something that many people with the ability to hear may take for granted but how amazing it is that she learned to speak! Think about trying to modify what you're saying until it's meaningful when you can't hear yourself. Keller shared that the "impulse to utter audible sounds had always been strong within me. I used to make noises, keeping one hand on my throat while the other hand felt the movements of my lips. I was pleased with anything that made a noise and liked to feel the cat purr and the dog bark."

-An alumna of Radcliffe College, she became the first blind/deaf person to earn a Bachelor of Art degree.

-She learned German, French, and Latin

-She penned her autobiography, The Story of My Life

-In 1915, she founded Helen Keller International, an organization dedicated to eradicating preventable blindness by providing health and nutrition education as well as free vision screenings and prescription eyeglasses to students living in poverty in the United States.

-In 1920, she helped found the American Civil Liberties Union, committed "to defend and preserve the individual rights and liberties that the Constitution and laws of the United States guarantee everyone in the country."[2]

What a story! What a feat! If Helen Keller could survive against all odds to live a productive and purposeful life what is holding you back from accomplishing your life goals? What obstacles are standing in your way to fulfilling your purpose and actualizing your dreams? You can overcome them all if you don't faint. Those who faint in times of adversity do not accomplish anything of worth in their lifetime and when they die, they are quickly forgotten. That is why you must not faint in the face of adversity. The bible says:

If you faint in the day of adversity, thy strength is small.
(Proverbs 24:10 KJV)

You need strength to overcome the travails of life. If you feel like the troubles of life are overwhelming you and that you have been pushed to the wall, do not quit; all you need is more courage, a little more faith, and some strength and determination. You need strength to scale the hurdles of life. You can draw strength from people like Nick Vujicic and Hellen Keller whose stories you have just read. You can also draw strength from motivational videos on YouTube or look back to previous challenges that you conquered and be inspired. You can seek help from friends or professional counsellors. And if you are a believer in Christ, you can pray to God for strength to enable you to overcome your hurdles. The Bible tells us of the unique strength we can get if we are connected to God:

But they that wait upon the Lord shall renew their strength; they shall mount up with wings as eagles; they shall run and not be weary, they shall walk and not faint.
(Isaiah 40:31 KJV)

These verses encourage us to look to God for help instead of quitting and giving up on life. With God on your side, your strength becomes renewed, you mount up with wings like eagles and you soar above your challenges. When your strength is renewed, you do not faint in the day of adversity, you run and do not get weary, and you leap over hurdles. With God on your side, your challenges cannot conquer you, you conquer them. David, the warrior King in the Bible, understood it better when he sang:

For by thee I have run through a troop; and by my God have I leaped over a wall.
(Psalms 18:29 KJV)

Focus on Your Dreams

One reason people give up too quickly in the face of obstacles is they completely take their eyes off their dreams and purpose and focus on the hurdles. That is a very easy way to be defeated in the journey of life. When you focus on your problems, they become magnified and appear insurmountable and you soon begin to give excuses why you do not think that you can overcome them. Satan uses the obstacles, hindrances, your past mistakes and other distractions to try to trick you into believing that you are done for and that there is no need whatsoever to continue to chase your dreams and move towards your destiny. If you speak with many mediocre people who gave up on their dreams and life pursuits, you will probably hear them say, they gave up because they didn't believe that they could still make it; they gave up because they lost hope in the beauty of their dreams.

No man actualizes his dreams if he loses focus of them and concentrates on his problems. Those who succeed and get to their glorious destiny are the people who despite the travails and bottlenecks trying to hinder them, set their gaze on the beauty of their dreams and the glory that would accompany achieving those dreams. Wife of a former president of the United States and a one-time head of the Red Cross Eleanor Roosevelt states it clearly:

The future belongs to those who believe in the beauty of their dreams.
-Eleanor Roosevelt

I learned from the life of Jesus Christ, that when troubles and the difficulties of life make a resolve to crush us, we should focus on the future and the joy that would come when we eventually actualize our dreams and reach our destination and then cultivate endurance, perseverance and the never-give up spirit. The bible says:

Looking unto Jesus the author and finisher of our faith, who for the joy that was set before him endured the cross, despising the shame, and is set down at the right hand of the throne of God (Hebrews 12:2 KJV)

Your cross might not be a physical one like Jesus' but you are sure to have a kind of cross; we all have our crosses that we will carry on our way to destiny. Your cross might be sickness, failure in business, childlessness, delayed university admission, delayed or failed marriage. It doesn't matter; what does matter is that you do not let it stop you from focusing on and achieving your dreams and life's purpose. Just like Jesus, look at the joy of you reaching your promised land and endure the pain, despise the shame. You will win if you don't quit.

When I was done with secondary school and was ready to go to university, I didn't know that there would be hurdles that would try to hinder me and delay me. I thought it would be a seamless journey. I was wrong; it was a rough one for me. As intelligent as I was, passing all my secondary school exams and being the laboratory prefect, I thought sitting for and passing the university entrance exam would be a walk in the park. I only realized that the road to achieving dreams is not an easy one after I had written and failed the entrance exam for the second time. I almost gave up and quit pursuing my education, but I was reminded in my spirit that quitters never win, and winners never quit. I made up my mind that I would keep trying until I gain admission. In the meantime, I decided to be actively involved in music, ministry, marketing of religious books and tapes and teaching children instead of allowing my failure to get admission to weigh me down. I also learned computer skills within that waiting period. Instead of being bitter with life, I had to get involved in other productive and soul-lifting ventures because as rightly put by Thomas Edison:

Everything comes to him who hustles while he waits.

With the help of my dad, I did not lose focus of my dreams of going to the university, as he constantly reminded me of the need to continue my educational pursuits. Eventually, I was admitted to study Economics at Lagos State University in Nigeria and I graduated after 4years with a second-class upper degree.

Had I given up and lost focus, I would not have continued my education nor would I have become a graduate. The lesson I want you to learn from my story is that when you are faced with life's hurdles and challenges, do not quit, or lose focus of your dreams. Fix your eyes on them and keep on trying until you eventually break through.

I would like to remind you that the bottlenecks on your way to destiny are surmountable. It is true that life is full of adversity and only the strong survive. If you do not faint but rather renew your strength, your hope and focus on the future ahead, you will overcome them all to reach your desired destination.

Nuggets

- As we walk towards our life's purpose and the fulfilment of our dreams, ambitions and life's goals, we must be reminded that we live in a world of difficulties and that we would and that hurdles, setbacks and bottlenecks are in the way.

- The greatest challenges of life are often encountered on our way to destiny. These challenges come as bottlenecks to try to convince us to give up and surrender our pursuits; they come to make us believe that we are not good enough and that we lack what it takes to achieve our dreams and fulfil our calling and purpose.

- Only those who understand that life is full of adversity and can adapt to the crushing circumstances of life, keep moving against all odds towards the realization of their dreams and purpose.

- Because you live in this world of adversity, life is going to try to crush you. You will encounter not-so-favorable conditions that you never envisaged, some of your dreams and ambitions will be threatened and your life's purpose will be tested by the trials of life. Unless you learn to adjust and adapt, you will most likely give up and settle for less.

- In the game of hurdles, you do not quit when you meet a hurdle, you leap over it. Hurdles are not meant to stop us; they are meant to be jumped over. With every hurdle you meet on your life's journey, your first instinct shouldn't be to quit but to jump over it.

- Those who faint in times of adversity do not accomplish anything of worth in their lifetime and when they die, they are quickly forgotten. That is why you must not faint in the face of adversity.

- If you feel like the troubles of life are overwhelming you and that you have been pushed to the wall, do not quit; all you need is more courage, more faith and more strength.

- One reason people give up too quickly in the face of obstacles is that they completely take their eyes off their dreams and purpose and focus on hurdles. That is a very easy way to be defeated in the journey of life.

- When you focus on your problems, they become magnified and appear unsurmountable and you soon begin to give excuses why you cannot overcome them.

- No man actualizes his dreams if he loses focus **of** them and focuses instead on his problems. Those who succeed and get to their glorious destiny are those who despite the travails and bottlenecks trying to hinder them, set their gaze on the beauty of their dreams and the glory that would accompany achieving those dreams.

Chapter Three
THE TRAVAILS OF MY YOUTH

The travails of life come in various forms and at different stages of our lives. Some people experience the greatest travails in their childhood. For others it comes in their teenage years, while they are still a youth or in adulthood. There are also people whose travails are lifelong, and they bear the burden that comes with it for the whole of their lives. Such lifelong travails could be a medical condition that is incurable, certain physical disabilities because of trauma or accidents, or inherited diseases. There are also certain unpalatable events that have a lifelong effect and make some people suffer the consequences if they are not able to overcome them and move on. A child who is sexually molested may bear the trauma for the rest of her life as the psychological effect of such abuse may lead to a promiscuous lifestyle in her adulthood, a lack of trust and hatred for men, or even a change in sexual orientation. A youth who is a victim of rape, for example, may bear that shame and feeling of violation and worthlessness for the rest of her life, if she is not able to heal from it. A teenage boy who loses both parents to a car accident and is unexpectedly now an orphan may for lack of parental care and guidance become a street boy and join bad gangs; he may even become an armed robber or a cultist if there is no one to play the father figure and motherly role in his life.No one can predict what lifehas in store for him and not all bad situations have a ready-made solution.

In this chapter, I shall be sharing my story and those of other people who experienced very unpalatable life circumstances. We shall also examine how the people got healed and moved on with life.

Broken but I am Healed

There are certain travails of life that completely break you and make life seem meaningless. You begin to wonder if there is any point in living and you ask why life is so unfair to you. "Why would life single me out to experience such pains?" you may ask! Such crushing events might sometimes lead to suicidal thoughts and many people have taken their own lives because they could not heal from the brokenness, they felt in the midst of their trials. I probably would have been one of such persons had God not helped me heal from the travails of my youthful days.

As a youth, I was fervent in spirit and committed to the things of the kingdom of God after I gave my life to Christ. I attended all necessary spiritual gatherings; conferences, prayer meetings, camp meetings, crusades, bible studies, and leadership trainings. I preached the gospel, ministered in songs, taught and mentored others in the way of the Lord, helped take cities for God, and did everything right that was required of a firebrand Christian.I also sold Christian materials: books, magazines and CD.I felt because I was that committed to the things of the Lord, that I was immune to the travails of life and that no evil could befall me. I confessed the scriptures and recited verses over and again that made me believe that nothing bad could happen to me. Nothing prepared me for the bitter experiences that followed. They almost broke me.

One early morning, I had just closed from an all-night church prayer meeting and was about going home when some armed men accosted me and forcefully had carnal knowledge of me. I was held against my will, stripped naked and raped at gunpoint. Before I could regain my composure, my molesters had fled. I was in pain, traumatized and completely broken. I was in tears, full of shame, humiliation and guilt. I blamed myself, blamed God, and asked why life was so unfair to me. I felt the most important part of my life; my innocence had been stolen and that there was no need to continue living or serving God. For the next few years, I became cold and lost interest in ministry and church activities. Had God not come to my rescue, I would probably have lost my faith and given up on life completely.

It took some years of study, mentorship, and self-development to gradually heal from my brokenness. It is true that I was broken, but I got healed. I later realized that my violation was for a reason. It was part of the trial of my faith and a test to prepare me for the great future that God had for me. Some passages of scriptures illuminated my spirit and encouraged me to move on with my life faster. One of the scriptures that I held on to through my healing journey was Apostle James' writing which says:

"Dear brothers, is your life full of difficulties and temptations? Then be happy. For when the way is rough, your patience has a chance to grow. So let it grow, and don't try to squirm out of your problems. For when your patience is finally in full bloom, then you will be ready for anything,

strong in character, full and complete."
(James 1:2-4 TLB)

From the verses above, I realized that as believers, we are not immune **to** the travails of life and that no matter how committed we are to the things of God, our faith would need to be tested. When your life is full of difficulties as a Christian, don't hate God or feel abandoned; instead, be happy! "How could I be happy in the face of difficulties and trials?" you may ask. The scriptures say you should count it all joy when you face diverse trials and troubles. The reason is that your trials and travails help you to cultivate patience and when that patience is complete, you will be strong in character and fully equipped for the journey to your destiny and the obstacles that would try to stop you. That was exactly what happened to me; my experience taught me patience, forgiveness, and perseverance, and gave me strength to overcome any other obstacle that I met on my way to my destiny. It also helped me to develop an unbreakable spirit.

Living with an Unbreakable Spirit

The travails of my youth made me understand that I was stronger than I thought I was. They revealed my own inner strength to me which I didn't know I had. After healing from my brokenness, I began to live with a new doggedness, and a never-give-up spirit. I **was** determined that nothing would break me again in my lifetime. I was ready to face the challenges of life head-on and fight for my destiny. My experiences became clearer to me when I discovered that some of the great ministers of God who are changing the world and impacting it positively for God had worse experiences than I had and yet didn't give up on life. I researched the lives of Joyce Meyer, Paula White, and a host of other internationally renowned preachers and realized that it seems, the greater your future and purpose, the more travails you would suffer on your journey to getting there.

For Joyce Meyer, her story was a bitter one and she is an example of recovering from abuse to living with an unbreakable spirit. Let me share her story with you:

Evangelist Joyce Meyer's powerful testimony of forgiveness is reaching thousands of people around the world.

Forgiveness has been a hard lesson for Meyer to learn. It is one based on years of sexual abuse at the hands of her alcoholic father.

"My father did rape me, numerous times, at least 200 times," she said during an interview. "There was no place I ever felt safe growing up."

"Literally, what he did was rape me, every week, at least once a week, until the time I was 18. My father, whom I was supposed to be able to trust, who was supposed to keep me safe, raped me a minimum of 200 times," she said.

While her childhood left her traumatized, Meyer has found restoration through her relationship with Jesus. She has a global ministry and most of all, a loving husband, and children. She also says she has forgiven her father for what he did to her.

But as she explains in a video posted to her Facebook page, there were times when she wondered where God was amid her abuse.

"Where was God in all this? Let's talk about that for a minute," Meyer tells the audience.

"I can't explain it to you in my mind...I know that God didn't get me out of it, but he did give me the strength to go through it. God had a plan," she said.

"About three years ago, I said that 'But of course, I wish I had not been abused' and God stopped me. He said, 'Stop saying that.' And then I thought about it, and I thought, and I know this sounds crazy, but I'm glad it happened. Do you know why? Because I'm a better person now than I ever would have been," Meyer tearfully explained. "I don't know how to make any sense out of that, but I know that God has redeemed me, and he has taken what Satan meant for harm and worked it out for good."

Many audience members were visibly moved and crying along with Meyer as she shared her story.

"I'm stronger. I know God better. I understand people's pain. And I believe it's made me able to reach out to you in your pain and your need and to tell you **with** all passion, God is alive," she said while pointing to her audience.

Meyer also tells the crowd that she is living proof that recovery is possible.

"Can you recover? You're looking at somebody who did. Amen? You're looking at the evidence that you can recover," she said. "There's no pit so deep that He can't reach down and lift you out of. He will set your feet on a rock. He will give you a wonderful life. He will give you beauty for ashes, the oil of joy for mourning, the garment of praise for the spirit of heaviness. He will make you a tree of righteousness, the planting of the Lord that He may be glorified."[3]

From Joyce Meyer's testimony, you could easily see that her case was a very bitter one because it was her father who molested her; not once, not twice, but over 200 times! How could she have survived that if not for the strength of God and her desire to not let the things that happened to her truncate her life's purpose? Today, Joyce has and is still impacting millions of people around the world and helping others who are going through the pain and travails of life. Perhaps you do not know Joyce Meyer and what she has made of the travails of her life. Here is a short biography:

Joyce Meyer is one of the World's leading Bible teachers and speakers who has her own syndicated television and radio program called "Enjoying Everyday Life". She is the leader of Joyce Meyer Ministries worldwide. She is a New York Times bestselling author, and her books have helped millions of people find hope and restoration through Jesus Christ. She also has a magazine titled "Enjoying Everyday Life".

Joyce started as a local Bible teacher in 1976, then became an associate pastor of a church in St. Louis, Missouri in 1980. She became an ordained minister in 1981. In 1985 her ministry was titled "Life in the Word".

By 2003, Joyce's ministry grew by leaps and bounds and soon she was teaching citywide, statewide, countrywide and now worldwide through Joyce Meyer Ministries and her television, radio and magazine titles were changed to "Enjoying Everyday Life". She teaches on hundreds of subjects based on her experience and how she applies the Bible to every facet of her life.

Joyce holds an earned Ph.D. in theology from Life Christian University in Tampa, Florida, an honorary doctorate in Divinity from Oral Roberts University in Tulsa, Oklahoma, and an honorary doctorate in Sacred Theology from Grand Canyon University in Phoenix, Arizona.

Joyce has authored over 90 self-help non-fiction books and a handful of fiction books.
Joyce was abused by her father growing up and by her first husband. Through God's Word, she was able to forgive these men. Joyce is a breast cancer survivor. She believes and teaches that regardless of a person's

background or past mistakes, God has a place for them and can help them on their path to enjoying everyday life.

Joyce and her husband, Dave, have been married for over forty years, and they are the parents of four grown children. Dave and Joyce Meyer have their home in St. Louis, Missouri. All four of Joyce's children are involved in some facet of Christian ministry.[4]

I wish every one of us could learn just like Joyce Meyer to not let the travails of life put an end to our life's journey, purpose, and calling. If we resolve to live with an unbreakable spirit no matter the bitter experiences, pain, sorrow, **or** past mistakes in our lives, we will heal faster and go on to live a purposeful and impactful life. Those who heal from their pain and brokenness usually become stronger, wiser, and more purposeful as they move towards their destiny. But those who allow the troubles of life to weigh them down and truncate their destiny, live a pitiable life; they make **little or no** impact, live a mundane life, and **leave** no legacies behind when they die. As I mentioned earlier, it seems the greater your future, the more troubles you would face in this life. Another story that made me reach that conclusion was that of Paula White.

For Paula White, her life and ministry suffered huge travails.

White, who calls herself the "former messed up Mississippi girl," faced a lot of scandals dating back to 2004; when a nine-year investigation was launched by the IRS into the personal and organizational finances of White and her then-husband, Randy.

The following years brought White face to face with numerous challenges to the point where she wanted to quit. She went through many tests and trials. A divorce, an alleged extramarital affair, a stroke, an addiction to the prescription medication she was given following her stroke, and having her church staff split down the middle, with some turning on the Whites and going to the media. She also encountered family problems that started when she found out that her son had a drug addiction and was sexually abused by another male at a staff member's house. White had to deal with the pain of her daughter, Kristen, battling brain cancer from which she died at age 30 in 2008.

In addition to all of this, White was still expected to preach, prophecy, and play her role in the church. It was "that kind of pressure" and "in a really weak moment" that she and her husband made the decision to divorce in 2007. The split was amicable.

White is a walking testimony that what the devil meant for bad, God turned into good.[5]

We could see from all the challenges White went through that she could have been broken but she never allowed her brokenness to stop her life's purpose. She healed from it and continued to live with an unbreakable spirit.

Today, Paula White-Cain is the president of Paula White Ministries, headquartered in Apopka, Florida. She is the Senior Pastor of City of Destiny Church and hosts the Christian television program Paula Today. Paula is a renowned life coach, bestselling author, and highly sought-after motivational speaker. Her commitment to humanity is felt worldwide as she reaches out through numerous charities and compassion ministries, fulfilling her mission and call to transform lives, heal hearts, and win souls.[6]

Who says you cannot overcome the travails of life and live a purpose-driven life? You can become what God has created you to be irrespective of the many challenges and troubles you would face in this life. All you need to do is to understand that travails are not **meant** to destroy you but to prepare you for a great destiny.

Before we conclude this chapter, I would like to highlight a few advantages of going through trials and life's travails.

- They build patience in you.
- They make you stronger.
- They make you wiser.
- They make you more courageous.
- They make you easily relate **to and** understand the pains of others and how to help them.
- They teach you caution.
- They prepare you for your purpose and destiny.

It is my belief that having read my story and those of Joyce Meyer and Paula White, you would not faint in your days of trouble nor give up completely on life. Instead, you would embrace your pains, learn the lessons that need to be learned from them and live the rest of your life with an unbreakable spirit as you walk towards your destiny and purpose.

Nuggets

- While there are certain unpalatable events that are themselves not lifelong, we may suffer the consequences for the rest of our lives if we are not able to heal from them and move on.

- As believers, we are not immune **to** the travails of life, and no matter how committed we are to the things of God, our faith would need to be tested. When your life is full of difficulties as a Christian, don't hate God or feel abandoned; instead, be happy!

- Your trials and travails help you to cultivate patience and when that patience is complete, you would be strong in character and fully equipped for the journey to your destiny and the obstacles that would try to stop you.

- It seems, the greater your future and purpose, the more travails you would suffer on your journey to getting there.

- If we resolve to live with an unbreakable spirit no matter the bitter experiences, pain, sorrow, and past mistakes in our lives, we will heal faster and go on to live a purposeful and impactful life.

- Those who heal from their pain and brokenness usually become stronger, wiser, and more purposeful as they move towards their destiny. But those who allow the troubles of life to weigh them down and truncate their destiny, live a pitiable life; they make no impact, live a mundane life, and **leave** no legacies behind when they die.

Chapter Four
I AM NOT A VICTIM

I t is often established that because of the travails of life and the inability to heal from them and move on with the pursuit of purpose and destiny, most people live the rest of their lives with the mindset of a victim. They begin to see themselves as victims of circumstances and live a pitiable and beggarly life going forward. With such mentality, they seek sympathy from others and appreciate it when people pity them. Instead of looking forward to the actualization of their life's goals and purpose, they are comfortable in mediocrity and define themselves by the circumstances and ugly events of their past. Unless a man eliminates the victim, mentality and stops defining himself by the travails or mistakes of his past, he will never be able to move into a glorious future and fulfil his life goals and purpose. This chapter focuses on the need to do away with the victim's mindset and emphasizes why it is better to focus on the visions, dreams and future ambitions, rather than on past mistakes and failures.

I am Not My Past

We all have our pasts; we all have made mistakes or experienced ugly and painful life circumstances in the past. But the greatest mistake you would make on your way to destiny is to allow your past circumstances to become your identity. When you identify yourself by your past, you lose your real identity and lose focus of your visions, dreams, and purpose. It is true that people may identify you by your past mistakes and ugly circumstances; they may even describe you by the travails of your past, by saying things like "that woman that had a divorce, that childless woman, that girl that was raped, that poor family, or that disabled man, that girl that got pregnant out of wedlock. Labeling a person by past events that hurt them is an error; you must never identify yourself by any of those traumatic situations. You have a name, an identity, and a purpose; so, do not allow anyone give you a false picture of your identity just because of the travails and mistakes of your past. The very moment you begin to see yourself as a victim of life's circumstances and join others to identify yourself by your problems, you set yourself up for a life of perpetual failure and mediocrity and there are only very few chances that your life would amount to anything great and worthy of emulation. A life-changing Speaker, bestselling Author, and

Behavioral Science Academic, Steve Maraboli has a perfect understanding of the situation. He writes:

"You are not a victim. No matter what you have been through, you're still here. You may have been challenged, hurt, betrayed, beaten, and discouraged, but nothing has defeated you. You are still here! You have been delayed but not denied. You are not a victim; you are a victor. You have a history of victory."

There is no great or successful person who did not at some point in his life encounter problems or make mistakes. Yet, they became great and successful because they did not allow the circumstances of the past to become their identity and stop them from pursuing their purpose and dreams. The secret to living beyond the circumstances of your past and walking into your glorious destiny is to quickly eliminate the victim's mindset and not let your past become your identity. You are not your past; you are what God created you to be. God sees your future and doesn't identify you by your past. He is more concerned about the great future ahead of you than your past mistakes and problems. That is why the scripture admonishes us to remember not the things of the past:

"Remember not the former things, nor consider the things of old.
Behold, I am doing a new thing; now it springs forth, do you not perceive it?
I will make a way in the wilderness and rivers in the desert.
(Isaiah 43:18-19 ESV)

People identify themselves by their past and live as victims for the rest of their lives because they are focused on their past instead of on their future. God says do not remember the former things or consider the sufferings of the past. He says He is doing a new thing in your life. You should let go of the past and begin to identify yourself by the great future ahead of you. You are not your past. It is true that you had a divorce, but that is not your identity. You may have had a failed marriage but that doesn't mean you are a failure in life and should live as one who is discouraged. No, you are not the things that happened to you in your past. You may have been raped in the past, but that is not your identity; you may have been childless but that is not your identity, for in the twinkle of an eye, a childless woman can become fruitful and have many children. The scriptures underlie this possibility:

"Sing, barren woman, who has never had a baby. Fill the air with song, you who've never experienced childbirth! You're ending up with far more children than all those childbearing women." God says so! "Clear lots of ground for your tents! Make your tents large. Spread out! Think big! Use plenty of rope, drive the tent pegs deep. You're going to need lots of elbow room for your growing family. You're going to take over whole nations; you're going to resettle abandoned cities. Don't be afraid—you're not going to be embarrassed. Don't hold back—you're not going to come up short. You'll forget all about the humiliations of your youth, and the indignities of being a widow will fade from memory. For your Maker is your bridegroom, his name, God-of-the-Angel-Armies! Your Redeemer is The Holy of Israel, known as God of the whole earth. You were like an abandoned wife, devastated with grief, and God welcomed you back, like a woman married young and then left," says your God.
(Isaiah 54:1-6 MSG)

I believe you can see from these prophetic verses why you should never identify yourself by your problems or live with a victim's mindset. The barren woman is going to have more children than the fruitful woman. Her circumstances would change for good and she will never remember the shame of her youth anymore. Glory to God! There is far more greatness ahead of you than the travails of your past. Walk with your shoulders squared and your head held high and live like you are already in that great future. Do not live in the past like a victim; live in the future like a victor. For the travails that you are going through now will not last forever. They are but for a moment. The sufferings of these present times are not worth be compared with the glory which shall be revealed in your future. So, God wants you to **look to** the future instead of the past.

That **is** why while Abram was still childless, God changed his name to Abraham to reflect the future He had prepared for him. Abraham means 'Father of many nations" How could God call a childless man the father of many nations? It is because God doesn't see us or identify us by our current or past circumstances, He sees us for who we could be, for our purpose and great destiny. It is for the same reason that God called Gideon "a mighty man of valor" while Gideon was complaining of being the least in his family and from the weakest tribe in Israel. Most people are not able to achieve much in life because they, just like Gideon, see themselves as victims of life circumstances and live with the victim's mindset. If we could see ourselves as God sees us and not live as victims, we would outdo our former selves by how much we would achieve and actualize in our lifetime.

It is time to break free from the victim's mentality and create the future of your dreams. It is time to identify yourself by your visions, ambitions, dreams, and purpose. Your history is behind you; don't let it hinder your great future. Your past is supposed to inform your future, not deform it. It is time to move upward and forward! Steve Maraboli explains it this way:

"Today is a new day. Don't let your history interfere with your destiny! Let today be the day you stop being a victim of your circumstances and start acting towards the life you want. You have the power and the time to shape your life. Break free from the poisonous victim mentality and embrace the truth of your greatness. You were not meant for a mundane or mediocre life!"
Living with a Vision

Instead of focusing on the troubles in your life and allowing thoughts of your past circumstances to overwhelm you and impede your life's journey, cultivate a vision, an ambition, and a dream for your life. Your life will only become meaningful when instead of living in the past, you create a vision, a dream, and an ambition for your future. The pursuit of vision, dreams and ambitions puts your life on the course of a great destiny. The reason most people live like victims of circumstances is that they have no worthy goals, ambitions and dreams for their future and hence have nothing exciting to pursue that makes their life worth living. That is an easy way to live a life of mediocrity and live in the past instead of focusing on the future. If you therefore want to overcome the travails of life and live beyond the mistakes of the past, cultivate a vision for your life and spend the rest of your life living that vision. Pastor Sunday Adelaja, a man of God who saw the vision which invloved taking Europe for Christ describes it this way:

Vision must be seen as something so significant without which a life is not considered worth living.

Life without vision would be a life of regrets, mediocrity, and mundanity. No matter what your past or current circumstances are, develop a vision for your life if you want it to be meaningful. If not for vision, Nick Vujicic, Joyce Meyer, Paula White, and the other people we shall discuss in this book would have lived in mediocrity and would not have made any impact at all. They all had a vision for their lives that kept them going amid all the troubles and life travails.

In creating a vision for your life, make sure that your vision is big and meaningful. Most people cultivate very worthless or meaningless **visions** for themselves and when they encounter any little challenge on their way to actualizing the vision, they give up and abandon that pursuit. The meaningfulness and strength of your vision increases your willingness to keep pursuing it even in the face of challenges and hurdles. Do not create obscure visions; make sure they are clear and easily understandable. When your vision has clarity, it makes it easier for you to focus on it and measure its success. If you really want to push yourself to greatness not minding your past or present circumstances, create very big dreams for your life. When you dream big, the dream itself generates an unusual energy in you that makes you work hard and **be** determined enough to defeat the hurdles that will try to stop you from achieving it. Daniel Burnham was an American architect who dreamt of amazing buildings that would change the lives of people. He planned big buildings. Perhaps that's why he said:

"Make no little plans. They have no magic to stir men's blood and probably themselves will not be realized. Make big plans; aim high in hope and work..."

Your vision is the picture of the kind of future you see and would like to have. It is the world of possibilities that you see irrespective of the mess you are currently in and the travails of your past. Your vision is the limit-breaking prospects you see in your mind that energize you to live above your ugly life circumstances. So, make sure it is big, strong, and meaningful. When you focus on a big, meaningful, and strong vision, you set yourself up for a life of greatness and success. However, if you focus on your travails, you put yourself on the path to mediocrity:

"The end result of such a life that is focused on challenges and obstacles of life rather than on possibilities, goal-reaching and limit-breaking prospects is mediocrity and failures."

Says Precious Isafiade, author and motivator who was raised by a single mother but has inspired numerous people to live above limitations with great perspectives in her books.

When you have a strong and meaningful vision, you dedicate your whole life to it and would even be ready to die to actualize it if need be. You would not care about the challenges and difficulties you may meet on the way; you would be ready to sacrifice everything to achieve it. One way to write your name in the sands of time and create a legacy is to have a vision so big and meaningful that nothing can stop you from actualizing it. You would embrace hardship, trials, travails, and anything else to make it come to pass. Such was the vision of Nelson Mandela for South Africa and indeed the world at large. When we talk about not letting your past define you and striving against all odds to fulfill a vision, no better name comes to mind than Nelson Mandela.

Nelson Mandela's life and legacy is one to view with a sense of honor and accomplishment. What is important to his story however is not just the vision he had for the nation of South Africa, but the vision for what the world could become if the racist divisions of the past were not given room to flourish for profits. Mandela imagined a world where color did not affect the way he and people of color were seen or represented. The story of Mandela's life and the challenges he faced growing up in South Africa, as well as the brutal history that spawned Apartheid is an interesting reference.

Mandela was born during the First World War in 1918. His roots in leadership were deep due to his powerful family history. "Mandela came from royalty. He came from the Thembu people." His father named him Rolihlahla which translates to "pulling the branch of a tree" but its colloquial means "troublemaker." The first time he went to school, a white teacher asked, 'What is your name?' and he says, 'My name is Rolihlahla.' The teacher says 'No, what is your Christian name' and when Mandela says he does not have one, she gives him the name Nelson." Throughout his life, Mandela faces the truth of what it means to be an African in South Africa. In this example he is being renamed in class by a white teacher who did not want to take the time to learn his name and what it meant. Further on we will see him being punished and disciplined for taking leadership roles against an oppressive system all around him. How did such an oppressive system start in the first place?

According to history, "The people of South Africa lived peacefully within their borders as independent people, running their own businesses, and owning their land and governing themselves. Then, in 1652, the first Dutch settlers arrived at the Cape of Good Hope. Initially, the interaction between the Dutch and the local people was cordial. There was trade and intermarriage. However, things started to change when the Dutch decided to settle permanently at the Cape. Conflict arose when Dutch settlers commenced seizing Khoisan lands and cattle and it sparked the first war in which the Dutch were able to further conquer the indigenous Khoi and San peoples of South Africa. From there, the seeds of racial and racist relationships originate from the Dutch settlement at the Cape.

From then on, the rights and freedoms of the Africans were being limited in exchange for profits. "By the 1890's Cecil Rhodes had created the DeBeers Company, the company which monopolized diamond production around the world. So, Cecil Rhodes was dominating the diamond industry. He also established a big company to dominate the gold industry. And by the early 1900's, Cecil Rhodes had helped to pass a law which ended up with the Afrikaner government coming up with the Native Land Act of 1913, which took 93% of all the land in South Africa and gave it to the minority whites." Similar laws would be put in place which would further limit the Africans of South Africa into lower positions in the social stratosphere.

From 1936 to 1994, Africans had no voting rights in South Africa. In 1948 a white only general election saw candidate Daniel Malan run on the slogans of Apartheid, black danger, white supremacy; black subservience, as well as whites will always be bosses in South Africa. Malan's government came to power, and "that system of Apartheid "apartness" or "separate" legalized racist, segregationist, oppressive policies against the Africans of South Africa,".

Mandela was instrumental in seeking change to fight back against apartheid. As he rose the ranks of the African National Congress in Johannesburg, there were many challenges, including the fear instilled upon many of its leaders which often stopped them from taking more action.

In a famous case known as Nelson Mandela and others vs. The State in 1963-64, better known as the Rivonia Trial, Mandela provides a statement that convinces people that it is worth doing what needs to be done. This statement is important for the trajectory of South Africa as we know it and as he knew it at the time. In his autobiography "Long Walk to Freedom" Mandela writes:

I had been reading my speech (for over four hours), and at this point I placed my papers on the defense table and turned to face the judge. The courtroom became extremely quiet, I did not take my eyes off Justice de Wet as I spoke from memory the final words.

During my lifetime, I have dedicated my life to the struggle of the African people. I have fought against white domination, and I have fought against black domination. I have cherished the ideal of a democratic and free society in which all people live together in harmony and with equal opportunities. It is an ideal which I hope to live for and achieve, but, if need be, my lord, it is an ideal for which I am prepared to die.

The silence in the courtroom was now complete. At the end of the address, I simply sat down. I did not turn and face the gallery, though I felt all the eyes on me. The silence seemed to stretch for many minutes, but in fact it only lasted no more than thirty seconds. From the gallery, I heard what sounded like a great sigh. A deep, collective 'Mm' followed by the cries of women.

These excerpts from Mandela's biography could be interpreted as a direct statement of Mandela's vision for not only South Africa, but the world as we know it, *a place with peace and equality for all.* Mandela would eventually be sentenced to jail.

During his twenty-seven-year jail term, Mandela loses everything except his life. Anything a man could lose he lost it. He lost his law practice, freedom, and family. "His mother died while he was in jail, he could not attend her funeral. His son died in a car accident and again, he could not attend the funeral. Mandela sacrificed everything for the freedom of the people in South Africa," Even upon his release, when many thought he had become a sellout to the South African government, even though he rejected all offers for a conditional release, he continued to forge reconciliation between the races of South Africa with his leadership. He would later be elected as the President of South Africa in 1994 and he built a democratic and free society in which all persons lived together in harmony and with equal opportunities just as he had envisioned.

Mandela's legacy is one of humility, honesty, reconciliation, and humanity. When someone puts you behind bars for twenty-seven years, you miss your whole life. You do not watch your children grow up, and still, you come out of jail and shake their hands and proclaim this is a 'Rainbow Nation.' That is the classic Mandela!

"Mandela epitomizes the idea of Ubuntu meaning humanity, the idea of being humane. As the great South African Reggae legend, the late Lucky Dube, noted in a scathing critique of South Africa's

Apartheid regime in one of his songs, 'God created humankind in His image .... But He didn't say Black or White. Who are you to separate the people? Different Colors, One People; Different Colors, One People!'"

Amandla! Viva Mandela, Viva![7]

We can see that Mandela despite all the travails he went through and spending 27years of his life in jail did not give up on his vision of the kind of South Africa he wanted. He did not even allow the stigma of spending such a longtime in prison stop him from pursuing his vision for South Africa. Because he did not live with a victim's mentality, he believed that his vision could still be realized despite the pain and troubles of his past. And as you would expect, he eventually became the president of South Africa and actualized his vision for the nation. If Nelson Mandela, despite all the travails of his past could actualize his vision and not allow his past to define him, **you can too**. You can create a vision for your life and pursue it. Don't let your past define you, cultivate a vision for your future and work towards achieving it. You can achieve it if you believe it.

Nuggets

- It is often established that because of the travails of life and the inability to heal from them and move on with the pursuit of purpose and destiny, most people live the rest of their lives with the mindset of a victim. They begin to see themselves as victims of circumstances and live a pitiable and beggarly life going forward.

- Unless a man eliminates the victim's, mindset and stops defining himself by the travails or mistakes of his past, he will never be able to move into a glorious future and fulfil his life goals and purpose.

- We all have our pasts; we all have made mistakes or experienced ugly and painful life circumstances in the past. But the greatest mistake you could make on your way to destiny is to allow your past circumstances to become your identity. When you identify yourself with your past, you lose your real identity and lose focus of your visions, dreams and purpose.

- You have a name, an identity, and a purpose; so, do not allow anyone give you a false picture of your identity just because of the travails and mistakes of your past.

- The very moment you begin to see yourself as a victim of life's circumstances and join others to identify yourself by your problems, you set yourself up for a life of perpetual failure and mediocrity and there is only slim chance that your life would amount to anything great and worthy of emulation.

- God doesn't see us or identify us by our current or past circumstances, He sees us for who we could be, for our purpose and great destiny.

- If we could see ourselves the way God sees us and not live as victims, we would out do our former selves by how much we would achieve and actualize in our lifetime.

- The reason most people live like victims of circumstances is that they have no worthy goals, ambitions and dreams for their future and hence have nothing exciting to pursue that makes their life worth living. It is an easy way to live a life of mediocrity and live in the past instead of focusing on the future.

- One way to write your name in the sands of time and create a lasting legacy is to have a vision so big and meaningful that nothing can stop you from actualizing it.

Chapter Five
FINDING YOUR PROMISED LAND

Every one of us has a promised land- a place of impact, purpose and fulfilled dreams. Life is only meaningful when we live and function within our promised land. Outside of it, we struggle, live for survival instead of for purpose and get frustrated with life and its many troubles. This chapter teaches how each and every one of us can find our promised land and function therein.

Your Place of Primary Assignment

We live in a world that is structured in such a way to prevent us from experiencing, and even making us completely oblivious that there is such a place as our promised land- a place of purpose and impact. From the time we are born, our parents begin to think about the kind of schools we will attend as we grow and the type of courses we would study at university. Sometimes, we ourselves are conditioned by society to choose certain career paths that we consider very lucrative and prestigious. It is either we want to become medical doctors because we think it's lucrative and prestigious or we want to choose such a profession because our parents desire it for us. We are either pursuing a career in Law because there is no Lawyer in our kindred or because we know we will easily get a job if we qualify as such a professional. The examples are unending.

Nobody really cares to know what our primary assignment on the earth is and where we are to carry out that assignment. Schools and universities do not teach primary assignments and the need to discover them; they only teach mathematics, physics, biology, economics, and other subjects that prepare us for the labor market. So, we spend many years of our lives in schools and universities, but have no idea why we exist, neither do we know the essence of our being. We know nothing about our primary assignment. What a tragedy!

While it is good to go to school and learn about the sciences, arts, humanities, and social sciences, we would never really know the meaning and essence of our lives, if we do not discover and fulfil the purpose for which we were born. Every one of us exists for a purpose. That purpose is your primary assignment on the earth. While you can do many other things with your life, there is one special purpose for which God sent you here. Unless you find that purpose and carry out that primary assignment, you will never find true fulfilment and satisfaction. You may get a good job, earn a lot of money and own properties worth millions, but if you are not carrying out your primary assignment and functioning within your promised land, you will not feel truly fulfilled. Your primary duty on the earth is to find out your life's purpose and fulfil it.

No one truly becomes great who does not discover and fulfil his life's purpose.

"True greatness is measured by whether a man fulfils his purpose on earth. True greatness is not about money or fame. It is about becoming what you were born to be". Clement Ogedegbe

When you do not know your life's purpose, you would roam the earth like a wanderer and pay attention to whatever beckons on you. You would be here and there, and your life would not really make any meaningful impact on others.

When people do not know their life's purpose, they

easily give up on life when the troubles and travails of life come knocking. The only thing that makes life worth living in the face of challenges and ugly circumstances is the purpose of your being. You can hardly knock a man down and get him frustrated with life when is living and fulfilling his purpose. The fulfilment and joy that come with functioning in one's place of primary assignment trumps whatever obstacles and hurdles try to get in the way on our life's journey.

So, one secret to overcoming the travails of life is to find out your life's purpose and fulfil it. "How can I find my life's purpose?" you may ask. That is a very valid question as I understand that not too many people know how to find or discover the purpose of their existence. We mentioned that schools and universities do not teach it, the media hardly talks about it and even religious organizations emphasize more on going to heaven than teaching us how to fulfil our primary assignment on the earth. So, multitudes of people are roaming the earth without any knowledge of what they were born to do or how to discover it. Little wonder our world is chaotic!

Going back to the question of how to discover your life's purpose, it is important to state that there is only one person who can accurately tell without any doubts what your life's purpose is; and that is God Almighty-your creator! The creator of every product has a purpose in mind for which he creates the product even before he starts the process of creating it. In the same vein, before God made you and formed you in your mother's womb, he already gave you a purpose and only He can accurately tell with absolute specificity what the purpose of your life is. The Prophet Jeremiah heard God when He said:

Before I formed thee in the belly, I knew thee; and before thou camest forth out of the womb I sanctified thee and ordained thee a prophet unto the nations.
(Jeremiah 1:5 KJV)

Just like Jeremiah, you and I were carefully formed and ordained to fulfil a specific purpose before we came out of our mother's womb. If God could tell Jeremiah his purpose, He can tell us too howbeit, not in the same manner as He told Jeremiah. You may not hear an audible voice telling you about your life's purpose, but God will communicate it to you in several ways. So, how can you have a clue what your life's purpose is?

1.   *God may speak to you through dreams, visions, and revelations where you hear a clear voice like Jeremiah did.*

Many people have discovered their life's purpose through dreams, visions, and revelations. For the Biblical Joseph, it was dreams he had about his life's purpose. Paul the Apostle formally Saul, had an encounter on his way to Damascus in which he had a vision and heard God revealing his purpose to him. If you are sensitive enough to understand God's voice, he may reveal your purpose to you through dreams or visions.

2.   *God may put a passion inside your heart that draws you towards your life's purpose.*

What problems are you passionate about that **are** almost like an obsession? Your purpose will always revolve around solving a problem and making the world a better place. Whatever problem you so passionately want to solve that you constantly think about is likely the purpose for which you were born. God put that passion inside of you to help you identify your purpose. Bishop Thomas Dexter Jakes, preacher, pastor and businessman understands how passion relates to purpose:

"If you can't figure out your purpose, figure out your passion. For your passion will lead you right into your purpose".

3.   *Your Gifts and Talents are a pointer to your life's purpose.*

There is a reason you were born with that natural talent and can do easily what others find difficult to do. If you can discover your talents, they will lead you to your purpose. Maybe you are a talented singer, pianist, footballer, or surgeon, your purpose is around that talent.

In the book **Gifted Hands***,* the autobiography of Dr. Ben Carson, the story of one of the greatest surgeons in human history was told. Ben Carson, being a gifted surgeon achieved a medical feat that is considered one of the greatest medical breakthroughs in human history; the separation of conjoined twins. Before Ben Carson's breakthrough, medical science had the problem of successfully separating conjoined twins. Born for this purpose, Ben Carson pushed through all the travails of his life to accomplish what no one before him could accomplish. His journey to his purpose was not an easy one, but because he discovered early what his gift and purpose was, he overcame the travails of his life to reach it. Ben Carson's life story is very revealing.

Ben Carson was born in Detroit, Michigan, on September 18, 1951, into a very poor family. After his parents Sonya and Roberts Solomon Carson's divorce, he was raised alone by his mother who could not accurately read or write as she had only a third-grade education. Seeing her sons' poor academic performance in school, Sonya made them study harder and required them to read regularly and submit reports on the books they had read. Ben was determined to succeed and fulfil what he felt was his life's purpose, not minding the challenges surrounding his life and family. Soon, his hard work would begin to reflect in his results as he began to excel in school.

In 1969, Ben graduated with honors as the student 'most likely to succeed' from Southwestern High School, a public school in Detroit. Upon receiving his high school diploma, Carson gained a scholarship to Yale University where he studied and graduated with a B.A degree in psychology. He went on to follow his passion of wanting to become a neurosurgeon by enrolling into the University of Michigan School of medicine. He graduated in 1977 with his M.D degree and went on to train at Johns Hopkins University as an intern, completing his internship in General Surgery and residency in neurosurgery there.

As a neurosurgeon, Ben was so gifted and exceptional. In 1987, through a groundbreaking surgical procedure, Ben Carson successfully separated conjoined twins who were joined at the head.

Ben also performed several other groundbreaking surgeries throughout his career and authored several motivational books about his life story. He also created three foundations- the Carson Scholars Fund, the Ben Carson Reading Project, and Angels of the Operating Room to help give back to society and impact the world at large.[8]

His life story is proof that every one of us through our gifts and passions can impact the world greatly no matter the challenges and obstacles we find on our way to destiny.

4.   *Your Purpose is connected to your past experiences and circumstances.*

Oftentimes, the circumstances and experiences of our past are pointers to what we were born to be.

These experiences could either be good or bad experiences; it doesn't matter; they are there to prepare us for our future purpose. Have you considered why the events in Moses' childhood had him being born in Egypt, hidden in a basket on the river Nile, raised in Pharaoh's house by Pharaoh's daughter and eventually growing up to kill a brutal Egyptian taskmaster? It was because he was born to deliver the Jews from the oppression of Pharaoh in Egypt and lead them to their promised land-Canaan. All those past experiences were to prepare him for his purpose.

You too can look at your past experiences and discover your purpose out of them. Why did you suffer the things you suffered? Why did you go through that trauma? Why did you go through a divorce, suffer a rape, or barrenness? Why were you so involved in church and ministry as a youth? Why were you in the choir? Could it be you were born to be a music minister, a minister of the gospel, or one who would inspire and motivate many broken people through the ugly circumstances of your past? You must connect the dots to discover your purpose.

I discovered that my own life's calling is centered around impacting lives through music and the ministration of the word of God and giving hope to people who are going through the travails I had gone through in the past. All the experiences I had in the past were to prepare me for that purpose. We must all intentionally prepare ourselves for exploits if we want to fulfil our purpose or God would through the circumstances of our past prepare us.

Preparing Yourself for Exploits

While the first step to fulfilling your life's purpose is discovering it, you would still not fulfil that purpose if you were not prepared for it. It is one thing to know that you were born to become a surgeon, but it is another thing to study and go through the training required for becoming one. Too many people fall short in their pursuit of their life's purpose because they, after discovering what they were born to do, fail to prepare themselves for the task ahead. To do exploits when you get to your promised land, you must adequately prepare yourself for it as you journey towards it.

Growing up as a youth, I was actively involved in church and fully committed to the music ministry. I was in the choir and traveled to different church events with my choir singing and impacting lives through music. Wherever the General Overseer of my church was going to preach, I was there to sing and bless lives. That was the preparation I needed to do exploits in my calling as a music minister. I soon began to write my own songs after God told me at the age of 17 that I could write songs and that many people would be blessed through my songs. Since then, I have written over 50 songs and most of these songs come to me as inspiration from the scriptures or from the messages I listen to while a preacher is preaching. Many lives have been impacted by my songs and I give God the glory!

No one truly excels in his calling and purpose without preparation. As soon as you discover what you were born to do, start preparing yourself. You can start by researching that area of calling; **you need to ask yourself questions:**

What does it entail?
What do I need to excel in that area?
Who are the people that are already excelling in that area?
What can I learn from them?
What is their secret of success?
What principles do they operate by?

These are all questions that you must ask and find

answers to if you want to excel in your calling and purpose. You must study and gain as much knowledge as you can in your area of calling before launching out. Look for successful people in your field and do the following:

Learn under them.
Do an internship.
Attend their mentorship classes.
Read their books.

Listen to their tapes and imbibe all the principles of success that you can.

The importance of proper preparation cannot be overemphasized as it relates to fulfilling your life's purpose and doing exploits. Abraham Lincoln said:

"Give me six hours to chop down a tree and I will spend the first four sharpening the axe".

What can a dull axe do to a tree? Nothing much! Just as a dull axe has not much impact on a tree, so will you have little or no impact on your generation if you do not first take enough time to prepare yourself before launching into your purpose-your primary assignment? Preparation is key to success in ministry, in sports, in politics and in any area of life you can think of. Without preparation, people fail and live an average life with no one feeling their impact or influence. If you don't want to be mediocre in your area of purpose, prepare yourself today. It is not all the time that God would allow you go through circumstances that would prepare you for future exploits; hence you must intentionally and consciously prepare yourself.

Nuggets

- Every one of us has a promised land- a place of impact, purpose and fulfilled dreams. Life is only meaningful when we live and function within our promised land. Outside of it, we struggle, live for survival instead of for purpose and get frustrated with life and its many troubles.

- We spend many years of our lives in schools and universities but with no idea of why we exist and the essence of our being. We know nothing about our primary assignment. What a tragedy!

- While it is good to go to school and learn about the sciences, arts humanities and social sciences, we would never really know the meaning and essence of our lives if we do not discover and fulfil the purpose for which we were born.

- While you can do many other things with your life, there is one special purpose for which God sent you here on earth. Unless you find that purpose and carry out that primary assignment, you will never find true fulfilment and satisfaction.

- You may get a good job, earn a lot of money and own properties worth millions, but if you are not carrying out your primary assignment and functioning within your promised land, you will not feel truly fulfilled.

- When you do not know your life's purpose, you would roam the earth like a wanderer and pay attention to whatever beckons on you. You would be here and there, and your life would not really make any meaningful impact on others.

- When people do not know their life's purpose, they easily give up on life when the troubles and travails come knocking. The only thing that makes life worth living in the face of challenges and ugly circumstances is the purpose of your being.

- You can hardly knock a man down and get him frustrated with life when he is living and fulfilling his purpose.

- The creator of every product has a purpose in mind for which he wants to create the product even before he starts the process of creating it. In the same vein, before God made you and formed you in your mother's womb, he already given you a purpose and only He can accurately tell with absolute specificity what the purpose of your life is.

- Too many people fall short in their pursuit of their life's purpose because they, after discovering what they were born to do, fail to prepare themselves for the task ahead. To do exploits when you get to your promised land, you must adequately prepare yourself for them on your journey.

- What can a dull axe do to a tree? Nothing much! Just as a dull axe has not much impact on a tree, so will you have little or no impact on your generation if you do not first take enough time to prepare yourself before launching into your purpose-your primary assignment.

Chapter Six
THE POWER OF ASSOCIATION

Whether or not you will quickly heal from the pains of your past or overcome the travails of your life is largely dependent on the association you keep, the people you spend most of your time with and share your problems with. How we respond to life's troubles and **stand up** from a fall depends on, among other factors, the relationships that we keep. In this chapter, we shall look at how our association affects our success or failure as we journey through the hurdles of life to reach our destination.

Who is in Your Inner Circle?

"I think I need to go to the hospital," I mumbled into my best friend's shoulder as she hugged me. We were in her driveway. Snowflakes flurried around us. The air was bitter, and my face was numb. The tears forming in my eyes burned hotter than normal in the cold. It was the 1st of January, and the New Year was not looking too bright.

Four days prior, I had come within inches of carrying out my first suicide attempt. Recently diagnosed with Post Traumatic Stress Disorder (PTSD), my entire system felt overloaded. Flashbacks to horrific moments from my childhood and marriage were daily occurrences. I experienced panic attacks in which my entire body shook, and my vision blurred until I didn't even know where I was. I was confident that I had completely lost my mind and that no one anywhere could help me. I had given up. I felt like a burden to my loved ones. So, I turned to suicide. But, at the last minute, I hesitated.

In the moment of my attempt, I suddenly remembered the shock and pain I felt in April 2014 when I received the call that my grandparents were both dead. In the ensuing hours, the entire family learned that they died by murder/suicide at my grandfather's hand. They had been such an influential force in my life, often serving more as parents than grandparents. I thought of my brothers, with whom I am very close. I also remembered something a therapist had told me once: "Ultimately, suicide is your choice. But you can decide to put it off for one more day. Knowing you have the power over that choice can help you. Choose to live for one more day. See how that day goes." I thought of my friends. I thought that I owed them one more day. I owe myself one more day. I'd pushed through for this long, and I could do it for one more day.

I spent the next day working a normal shift at the group home, as I had done for the past five years. Despite my own battles with depression, it has always been far easier for me to support others with mental health struggles than to admit **to** my own. I don't remember any part of my shift on this particular day, though. I was operating completely on caffeine and autopilot. I felt disconnected. I couldn't think of anything other than the night before. Thoughts of suicide and desperation for relief felt all encompassing.

I had been sitting with these feelings alone for a month. I wasn't being fully open with friends or in therapy. Growing up in a home filled with abuse and instability, my defense mechanism has always been to minimize what I'm feeling. This is a common by product of chronic abuse. I was the "Caretaker" in my family. I felt the immense burden of being the one who "could handle things." I felt unable to express fear, sadness, or anger as it would often result in more chaos, abuse, and instability. The need to be "OK" in the eyes of others became one of the core values, albeit an unhealthy one, which I carried into adulthood.

When I called my best friend, Cassie, I intended to tell her everything over the phone, but all that came out was, "Hey, are you busy this weekend?"

Thankfully, she had no plans for the New Year beyond staying at home with her two children, so she invited me to come down with my daughter to spend the weekend.

Although I had not revealed all I had wished to over the phone, I did manage to buy myself more time. I knew I would not harm myself while with her. I also knew that she'd help me gauge the severity of the situation. Having known me for over fifteen years, I trusted her opinions.

It seems counterintuitive, maybe, but a part of me also thought I was overreacting. No matter how close I felt to the edge, a part of me honestly did believe that it wasn't as bad as it seemed or would sound to someone else. I knew that most people would hear the events of the previous night and call 911 immediately, but a portion of me was in complete denial, thinking that the previous night was just a one-off incident. Perhaps it had come and gone, and I could return to simply white-knuckling my way through this.

Having struggled with depression, anxiety, and insomnia for most of my life, and with suicidal thoughts since I was thirteen years old, on some level, this battle with PTSD simply felt like my normal issues cranked up a few notches. Sure, I was now also dealing with flashbacks and full-blown panic attacks, and, yes, the night before had been the closest I'd ever come to attempt suicide, but I asked myself, "Is this really any different than being fifteen years old, lying on my futon, and wishing I had a gun so I could just end it?"

The night before I had been calm. It felt completely natural to be sitting in a cheap motel room, where no one I cared about would find me, drunk out of my mind with a bottle of pills in my hand. I couldn't differentiate between passive and active suicidal thoughts. But my survival instinct was still intact, no matter how distant it felt, and it was screaming to be heard.

Once the weekend came and I arrived at Cassie's house, I asked to talk with her alone. I told her everything—the flashbacks, the nightmares, the fact that I hadn't had more than a few hours of sleep each night in over a month. I told her about the motel room and the pills and the drinking. I told her I didn't think I could keep going on like this. With a confidence that, in hindsight, scares me, I said, "I'm going to kill myself." I also told her emphatically that I did not want to go to the hospital.

Like many other people, I held negative expectations of what "being in a psych ward" would entail. I was terrified of being over-medicated, ignored, written off because I was "a crazy person," and dehumanized. Cassie saw the fear, heard the desperation, and picked up on the tension I felt awaiting her response. She simply hugged me at first, and, when she spoke, my fears about her response vanished.

"We're going to figure this out. We'll do some research, we'll make some calls, and we'll figure out what to do. You don't have to do anything you don't want. The second to last place I want you to end up in is the hospital. The last place I want you is the morgue."

I agreed with her plan because she was leaving the choice, ultimately, in my hands. At this time, when I felt completely out of control, she gave me agency. She also made it clear that she was right next to me, for whatever may come. I knew I was not "in it" alone anymore.

Over the weekend, she held me through panic attacks, talked me through grounding exercises during flashbacks, and comforted me after nightmares.

We called local crisis support and the National Suicide Prevention Lifeline. She did most of the talking on the phone calls because I was too ashamed and scared to explain the situation myself, but she kept the phone on speaker and sat next to me as she spoke, allowing me to speak when comfortable and make any corrections I felt necessary.

We searched Google for resources and any indication of when hospitalization was necessary. We talked together about options. We emailed my therapist. We did everything we could think of doing. Every resource said that I should be at the hospital.

Despite that, Cassie did not push. I asked her periodically what she thought, and she'd simply respond with "I know that you're not going to hurt yourself as long as you're with me, and I'm not calling 911."

Unspoken was the sentiment, because, ultimately, it's your choice to make. You are going to have to decide whether to go to the hospital or not, and until you do, I'm going to be here supporting you and keeping you safe.

And she did just that. She kept me safe for the entire weekend. It was almost time for me to go home, go back to work, go back to white knuckling it. The motel room was still at the forefront of my mind. A part of me knew, if I went back home, I would follow through. But the weekend with Cassie showed me that at least one person on this earth would be incredibly upset if I did. When she met me in the driveway on Sunday night, I imagine that she was relieved as I finally admitted, to myself and to her, that I needed to go to the hospital to stay safe.

I'd made the decision, but a large part of me was still in denial. I wasn't thinking clearly due to the lack of sleep. In the waiting room, I remember turning to her and saying, "You know, they just want to interview me. They could decide that I don't need to be here after all."

She agreed. Cassie knew from the multiple conversations with mental health professionals over the course of the weekend that I would be admitted, but she let me sit in the comfort of my denial for just a little longer. I needed it.

When I was called to the back quickly after checking in with a nurse, Cassie came with me. On the chair in the examination room, I saw a set of hospital clothes.

The nurse instructed me to put them on. I realized at that moment that I was going to be admitted. I felt relief that maybe there was hope. Maybe there was a chance of recovery. But I was overwhelmed by fear of the experience I imagined was ahead of me. Had Cassie not been there, I'm not sure I would have had the courage to stay. But she was there. And I knew she wasn't going anywhere, which meant I wasn't going anywhere other than a hospital room.

After an interview with a psychiatrist, blood work, and two hours of waiting, a doctor came in and said, "You would be a great candidate for our program if you agree. A typical stay is two or three days. We'll have you out and back to your normal life in no time. What do you think?"

Despite my anxiety, I agreed to voluntarily admit myself to the psychiatric unit. Once I agreed, the fear and relief collided with the stress of the past month and my hands began to shake. But there was an underlying comfort: there was no more uncertainty, no more denial, no longer need to be "OK"—the decision was made.

When the doctor left the room, I turned to face my best friend, I recalled us at thirteen years old, when we first became friends, our awkward punk rock phase, sleepovers that lasted for entire weekends, prom night with our respective dates, our weddings, and countless playdates between our own children. I wanted to thank her: to say something profound.

Instead, I said with a shaking voice, "Well, we always said one of us was going to end up in a psych ward. Now we know who."

She laughed. And her laugh made me laugh.

We waited in that room for seven hours before a bed was prepared for me. We alternated between joking and discussing the logistics of the situation.
While we were waiting, a woman in the next room began screaming "No!" and "Please stop!" This triggered a flashback of my mother being beaten by my stepfather. Cassie held me through that flashback. She let me speak when I wanted to and allowed silence when I needed it. She was there until they put me in a wheelchair and pulled me through the door labeled "Psychiatric Care."

Her unwavering acceptance of me, even at my worst, gave me the courage and ability to accept the truth: I needed help. Ultimately, it saved my life. Her ability to maintain a sense of normalcy helped me feel grounded.

My time in the psychiatric unit was not the horror story I thought it would be. It was a lot of group therapy and medication adjustments. It was helpful. It was also not a cure at all. I'm still fairly young in my recovery journey. In addition to PTSD, I've been diagnosed with bipolar disorder. My stay in the hospital lasted for seven days instead of the projected three. I was discharged into a month-long partial hospitalization program, and I accessed crisis stabilization care during another depressive episode in August. Now, I attend weekly therapy and monthly psychiatry check-ins.

I never would have connected with most of those resources, or made it this far in my recovery, had I not taken the initial step of voluntary admittance to the hospital. And I would not have taken that step without the love, support, and acceptance of Cassie.

She's been there every step of the way, and her faith in my ability to recover has given me faith in myself, faith in the professionals, and faith in recovery.

This is the story of Sheila O' Donnell.

Sheila O'Donnell is a Vermont based mental health advocate and blogger. She worked direct service mental health in a group home setting for 5 years, studied Social Work in college, and interned as a case manager at a local mental health agency. In January of 2016, she was admitted to a psychiatric unit following a manic episode and the emergence of severe post-traumatic stress symptoms. Since that time, she has been sharing her story, her perspective as someone who's been on "both sides of the aisle,"and helpful recovery skills and tools through her blog Parallel Dichotomy.[9]

From the story above, we could easily see how having the right friends could be one of the greatest secrets to quickly recovering from the travails and troubles of life. Had Cassie not been there for Sheila to give her the care, support and encouragement she needed to hold on to life, Sheila would probably have allowed the travails of life to make her end her own life.

Whether you like it or not, your ability to overcome life's travail and move on towards your purpose and dreams will hugely be influenced by the people you surround yourself with. You would hardly find a person who successfully recovered from heartbreak, a divorce, an abuse, a financial crisis, a mental health disorder or bereavement who was not in one way or the other helped by a friend or relative. No man is an island; we all need people to succeed, overcome life's challenges and become better in life. The man who isolates himself in times of trouble and tries to figure things out by himself would have a hard time conquering the travails of life and might be conquered by them himself. But he who reaches out will find help and a shoulder to lean on. That is why I completely agree with the lyrics of the song "lean on me" when it says:

Sometimes in our lives
We all have pain.
We all have sorrow.
But if we are wise
We know that there's always tomorrow.
Lean on me
When you're not strong
And I'll be your friend.
I'll help you carry on...
For it won't be long
Till I'm gonna need somebody to lean on
Please swallow your pride
If I have things, you need to borrow.
For no one can fill.
Those of your needs that you won't let show.
You just call on me brother when you need a hand.
We all need somebody to lean on
I just might have a problem that you'll

understand.
We all need somebody to lean on
-Bill Withers

If you want to overcome the travails of your life faster, find a trusted friend, colleague, relative to share your burdens with and have their shoulders to lean on. A problem shared is half-solved. There is no point dying in silence because of pride; it could lead to suicidal thoughts. We all have problems in our lives, and no one is immune from challenges. However, we are all not in problems at the same time. When you are strong, I might be weak and when you are weak, I might be strong. That's why you should not be ashamed to seek help from the people in your inner circle. You might find a shoulder to lean on and a solution to your problems when you open up.

While it is good to seek help from others, you must be careful who you share your problems with. Not everyone can help you recover and overcome life's challenges; some people might complicate things for you. They might discourage you, add salt to your injury, fuel your mind with negativity and do everything to make you stay down forever. That is why you must be very careful about the association that you keep. The quality of people in your inner circle can either make or mar you. It is a general principle of life that our success in life is greatly influenced by the association that we keep. Apostle David Zilly-Aggrey is Senior Pastor Royal House of Grace Church. He explains the importance of the association you keep:

"It doesn't matter whether we are talking about business success, leadership success or academic success, your association could be the major cornerstone of your success."

We can easily tell the outcome of a person's life and whether he would be able to overcome the travails of life by merely looking at the association he keeps. Who are your friends? Who are the people in your inner circle? Can they help you in times of trouble? Do they inspire you to succeed or discourage you? Are they fueling you with positive energy or with negative energy? These are vital questions that you need to answer.

As you journey towards your destiny, you would meet hurdles as well as people. You have to be very careful who you bring into your inner circle as a close friend. The people you surround yourself with will determine how far you can go on your life's journey and how well you can overcome the hurdles of life. This is because they can influence your personality, point of view, and your response to challenges. If they are fearful people that give up easily in the face of challenges, you too would soon become fearful and give up easily on your challenges. If they are courageous people with a *never-give-up spirit*, that is who you would most likely become. It is common knowledge that you become like the people you spend the most of your time with. So, imagine always being in the company of people who are good at playing the blame game and who instead of taking responsibility for the outcome of their lives, blame everyone else for their problems and never take a step to better their lives. It won't be long before you will start blaming others for your problems and you will take no actions to better your life. Instead, you would wallow in self-pity and play the victim's card.

I believe you can now begin to see that the people you surround yourself with as you journey through life can greatly determine whether or not you will overcome the hurdles on your way and reach your destination. The people in your inner circle can affect your thought pattern, inspire or demoralize you, and help you to fix your eyes on your goals or make you fix them on your problems. Just as Cassie helped Sheila overcome the travails of her life and her suicidal thoughts, so should your friends be able to help you in your time of troubles. This is a call to do an inventory of the people in your inner circle; change them if they are not inspiring, encouraging, helpful or making your life better. You deserve the best of friends around you.

Also make sure you have like-minded people in your inner cycle; people who have similar dreams and goals as you. Walk with people who are going in the same direction as you intend to go. If you keep company with people who are going in an opposite direction to yours or people who are not inspiring you to go in the direction of your dreams, you may not arrive at your destination or actualize your dreams because wrong friends could slow you down.

The Need for Mentorship

"If you cannot see where you are going, ask someone who has been there before."
—*J Loren Norris*

While it is good to carefully select your friends and the people in your inner circle if you want to quickly overcome the travails of your life and achieve your life goals faster, it is better to have a mentor. The problems and challenges you will encounter on your life's journey are not going to be peculiar to you; you probably won't be the first person to experience such circumstances. No trial or temptation has or will come your way that is not common to man. People have experienced divorce before, others have experienced financial crisis, heartbreak, diseases, poverty, homelessness, rape and domestic abuse before, and you would not be the first. In the same vein, the goals, and dreams that you want to achieve have probably been achieved by other people before. There is perhaps someone who is already walking and excelling in a similar purpose and calling as yours. These people are qualified to become your mentors and show you the way.

We overcome the travails of life faster when we let people who have conquered similar travails hold our hands and guide us through the steps to overcoming them. We actualize our goals, dreams and fulfil our purpose faster and easier when we sit under the tutelage and guidance of those who have already achieved something similar. You will have a hard time navigating the troubles of life and reaching your destination if you do not have a mentor. If you want to effortlessly overcome the travails of life and successfully reach your destiny, you need a mentor.

A mentor points you in the direction you should go and tells you where the bumps are on your way to destiny and shows you how to maneuver through them. With a mentor, you can be sure that your life's journey would be easier than it would have been if you were walking the difficult roads alone. It is true that there are bottlenecks to destiny, but your mentor knows where they are and can tell you how to avoid them. He is your mentor because he has experienced what you are currently experiencing and conquered. He has walked the path to his promised land-the place of purpose, dreams, and accomplished goals. He, therefore, can show you the way.

When God asked me to start *"Fight the Good Fight of Faith with Lola Ministry"*-an outreach program that I am going to talk about in a subsequent chapter, I didn't know exactly how to go about it and how to start the WhatsApp group. I needed a mentor to guide me and show me the way. Thankfully for me, I had previously been introduced by a friend to a WhatsApp group called *'Developing Women to Survive Empowerment Initiative' (DWSEI)*. While in the group, I met with the administrator, Mrs. Abimbola Onwuchekwa and spoke to her about what God had asked me to do. I told her that what she was doing was exactly what God wanted me to do but I didn't know how to go about it. She encouraged me and told me not to give up and that if God had asked me to do it, then I must do it. She took up the role of a mentor in my life from that day and made sure that I chose a specific date on which I would start my own WhatsApp group for my outreach *'Fight the Good Fight of Faith with Lola Ministry'*. She coached me and followed me up until the date I had chosen and made sure I opened the group on that day. She continued to mentor me and correct my mistakes after I opened the group until I learned how to properly manage it. That group has become a huge success and a source of blessing to many people since then. How would I have achieved that without the help of a mentor?

You need a mentor; I need a mentor; we all need mentors. Only a prideful person would say he doesn't need a mentor and that he can figure out life all by himself. Such a one would have a hard time overcoming the travails of life and actualizing his dreams. He might spend the bulk of his life trying and failing and just moving in cycles without making any meaningful progress.

Nuggets

- Whether or not you will quickly heal from the pains of your past or overcome the travails of your life is largely dependent on the association you keep, the people you spend most of your time with and those whom you share your problems with.

- How we respond to life's troubles and get up from a fall depends on among other factors, the relationships that we keep.

- Having the right friends could be one of the greatest secrets to quickly recovering from the travails and troubles of life.

- Whether you like it or not, your ability to overcome life's travail and move on towards your purpose and dreams will hugely be influenced by the people you surround yourself with.

- You would hardly find a person who successfully recovered from heartbreak, a divorce, an abuse, a financial crisis, a mental health disorder or bereavement who was not in one way or the other helped by a friend or relative.

- The man who isolates himself in times of trouble and tries to figure things out by himself would have a hard time conquering the travails of life and might find himself being conquered by them. But he who reaches out for help will find help and a shoulder to lean on.

- The people you surround yourself with will determine how far you can go on your life's journey and how well you can overcome the hurdles of life.

- If you keep company with people who are going in opposite direction to yours or people who are not inspiring you to go in the direction of your dreams, you may not arrive at your destination or actualize your dreams. As they could distract you and slow you down on your journey to success.

- We overcome the travails of life faster when we let people who have conquered similar travails hold our hands and guide us through the steps to overcoming them.

- You will have a hard time navigating the troubles of life and reaching your destination if you do not have a mentor.

Chapter Seven
LIFE POURED ALL IT COULD ON ME

After my rape experience and the trauma that followed which made me almost lose my faith in God and the things of the Kingdom, I thought **I had seen the** worst travail of my life and since I was able to recover from it and didn't lose my faith, that the rest of my life would be void of troubles and painful experiences. Little did I know that those travails of my youth were only the beginning of birth pangs, the beginning of sorrows, and that I was only being prepared for greater trauma and pain. This chapter sheds more light on some of the terrible events of my life that caused me so much pain and how I overcame them.

Trauma and Pain Multiplied

While in the third year of my university, I got married to a man with whom I had fallen in love while I was still a teenager. **We were dating for six years before marriage**. Around the time I first met him, I was already into business and excelling as a sawyer-a skill I learned from my mother who was also a sawyer. That business flourished so much in my hands that I made a lot of money from it and was the major supplier of timber to some of the big local and international companies back then in my state and beyond. I managed this business while studying Economics in the university. My fiancé, who later became my husband joined me in the business since it was not easy for me to combine school and business as my business required me to travel out of the state most of the time to strike deals and supply wood to clients. With the support of my fiancé the business grew and excelled even more.

After I got married, I handed over the leadership of the company to my husband since we were taught in church that the husband is supposed to be the head of the wife. I didn't know that decision would be one of the biggest mistakes of my life. Before I got married, I had an idea of what I thought an ideal marriage should be like; a loving, caring, forgiving and romantic relationship between two adults who are committed to each other for the rest of their lives and living in peace and harmony. Martin Lurther, the seminal figure of the protestant reformation worte:

"There is no more lovely, friendly, and charming relationship, communion, or company than a good marriage".

I was excited about getting married, hoping that my marriage would be heaven on earth and that I would be in the arms of a protective, loving, caring, kind and forgiving husband. It wasn't long after I got married that I realized that successful marriages take work, and that marriage comes with a handful of challenges and troubles. I however, did not envisage that mine was going to move from a healthy romantic relationship to one of abuse, strife, anger, quarrels, unforgiveness, sex deprivation and eventual divorce.

Soon after I handed over the leadership of my company to my husband, the challenges of marriage began to not only affect our marital relationship in the home but also our business. Sometimes, after I had struck a deal with a marketer that would earn us huge profits, my husband would because of a quarrel at home say we are not supplying to that client. I would feel very bad because it took a lot of energy and stress for me to successfully strike **such** a deal. Not wanting my efforts to be wasted, I would go on my knees and beg my husband to forgive me for whatever grudges we had and allow me supply products to our marketers. He would stand his ground and say No! And once he says no, it remains no. He was so rigid and unforgiving. On one occasion, we got a contract to supply products and my husband out of anger from our marital crisis said we would not execute that contract. After much begging and him remaining obstinate, I went to the bank to withdraw money to execute the deal. I was able to have access to the bank account because since the company was registered in my name before my husband joined me, I was the main signatory to the account. After withdrawing the money, I went to execute the contract. When I returned home, my husband gave me the beating of my life; I was like a primary school girl being flogged and disciplined by a schoolmaster. I never envisaged before I got married that I would one day become a punching bag in the hands of the man I expected to love and protect me. I don't think I would have survived such physical violence and rage had my landlord not come to my aid. I was bruised and traumatized. This was not the kind of marriage I signed up for. How could my husband brutalize me for executing a business deal that would bring huge profits to our company? It was not as if the profits were coming to me alone; they were going into our joint account. Because, I was so naïve at the time, I didn't have the wisdom to open my personal account; so, we operated a joint account. Yet, I still got the beating of my life for doing a job that would enrich both of us.

That singular event made me discouraged and lack interest in striking more business deals since I knew that all my hard work might be in vain if my angry husband disapproves of their execution. My husband was the kind of man that loves the silent treatment, and he could go for months without talking to me and forgiving me for an alleged offence. We would go for months without reconciling after a petty quarrel. It was a huge trauma for me living in the same house with such a man. You would have to experience it to understand how traumatizing and heartbreaking it is to live with a partner in the same house who loves **to stop communicating** for as long as his pride allowed him. Such negative energy greatly affected not only our relationship at home but also our business. It was not long before I eventually became a full-time housewife and left the business for him to run alone since he was now the leader. I always had to stay at home and go to work only when he needs me to. That was how we lived until a devasting event would change the course of my life.

While all this was happening, I had an elder sister called Bose who was living in Paris, France who knew about the trauma and pain I was going through in my marriage. She had relocated to France a long time ago but would often visit Nigeria to see the rest of us living in our home country. One day after attending my father's burial she had just left Nigeria for France and she called me and asked to know how I was doing. I told her I was fine even though I was broken and traumatized by my husband's cruel attitude towards me. She then told me she was aware that I wasn't happy in my marriage and asked if I would like to move to Paris. I declined and told her that I can't leave my husband in Nigeria and travel to Paris. I felt that since my husband was making me go through hell even though we were living together in the same house, he would do worse if I travelled to Paris and leave him behind in Nigeria. That would be good riddance to bad rubbish for him I said to myself! I declined the offer because I feared that my marriage and business might crumble if I lived apart from my husband. So, it was best for me to stay with him and bear the burden of what has turned into an abusive marriage. I thought Bose was merely asking me to come to Paris to take a break from the pain and suffering I was going through in my marriage until she told me she had breast cancer and would need me to come to help take care of her kids. I thought she was joking, and I told her that even if she had AIDS, I would not leave my husband and go to Paris.

The following day, my mother called me and said, "Bose needs your help, she is going through chemotherapy and she has two children that need minding; why don't you go and help her intermittently for the time being?" I felt so broken to know that my sister actually did have cancer. I was facing marital challenges, a failing business, bereavement from my father's demise and then my sister was down with cancer. "What a cruel life!" I said to myself. Although I really wanted to go and help my sister in France, I told my mum they would need to seek my husband's permission to allow me to travel. It is worthy of note that my husband was not having sex with me for that period because he was angry with me. Whenever he was angry with me, he denied me everything including sex. Sometimes, for five months, my husband would starve me of sex and never touch me. I would kneel down and beg him most nights to forgive whatever wrong he felt I had done that got him angry; yet he would not get intimate with me. I was seriously emotionally traumatized and in pain.

So, when he was told I needed to travel to France, he was so happy. He was like "yes, you should go, you know you like travelling, when you get to Paris, I will support you" He was so excited and took my international passport and said he would do everything to make sure I travelled. We then went to the French Embassy to submit the passport and apply for the visa. It was strange to me that my husband was happy I would be travelling and leaving him behind. There was something suspicious about his attitude and that gave me a lot of concern. Not fully convinced whether I was making the right decision to travel, I went to the embassy secretly to take back my passport and cancel the visa application. I got home with my passport and told them I was denied a visa.

Some weeks later, while I was working at a new job, I had just started with a multilevel marketing company, I came in contact with a client whose mother-in-law was a prophetess. While at her house, she told me her mother-in-law would like to see me. I obliged! When I met her, she asked why a young girl like me was doing that kind of Job and requested to pray for me. After praying, she told me that she saw a revelation in which I was among white people. That it looked like I was abroad. It was then I told her about my sister who had asked me to come to France to help her with her kids. I told her I refused to go because I didn't want to leave my husband behind. She then told me that if there is a need for me to travel, that I should not hesitate and that she saw me abroad in her revelations.

After that encounter, I called my sister Bose and told her I would come to Paris and that my mind was made up. She made sure I wasn't joking and after I assured her of my seriousness, we started a fresh visa application, and I eventually got the visa. This time, I didn't tell my husband about the new application until I got the visa. He said I should have told him before applying but that since I already got the visa, I should travel. I started preparing to travel and just two days before I would travel, my husband returned from work in the evening and in the darkness of the night asked me in the room if I was still travelling. I told him to put on the Generator first so we could have light because I was so scared that he might harm me. He kept on asking if I was still going to travel and out of fear, I told him that I was no longer travelling. I was so scared because that was the period, we were quarrelling that he would not have sex with me for five months despite all my pleas. So, asking me such a question in a dark room was scary for me. After I told him I wasn't travelling, he said OK! And that was it.

The following day, our Lawyer called and requested to see me at her office. I got there only to find my husband there. She then asked me before my husband if I was going to travel. I had to open up and said yes! My husband got furious and said he knew I lied to him. He then left the office and started making calls, telling people I was traveling. I do not know the people he was talking to on the phone. I had to tell my lawyer that I didn't feel safe being alone with my husband anymore since I do not trust his mental health. I told her I wasn't going forever; I was only going to help my sister who has cancer to take care of her kids.

When we eventually got home, I arranged my traveling bags and called my siblings to come to my house. I told my husband I would be going with them to their house since I no longer felt safe alone with him. Because I was scared of what he might do to me that night, I had to go spend the night at my siblings' house and traveled to Paris the following morning.

Paris Had More Troubles Waiting for Me

When I eventually arrived in Paris, I began calling my husband's phone, but he wouldn't pick up my calls. After several days of calling without a response, I was completely broken and began crying. My sister asked why I was crying, and I told her. She said I shouldn't worry that we would keep trying. I had to send my sister's and her husband's phone numbers and the landline to him hoping that someday he would call me, yet no response. The first week passed and no call or SMS from my husband. I became so frustrated and wondered if that would be the end of my marriage. I soon packed my things and told my sister I was going back to Nigeria, "I can't lose my marriage" I said to her. She asked me how I intended to go back to Africa and whether I knew my way from Europe to Africa. I told her my husband still wasn't picking up my calls and it's eating me up. She then asked me a question "what if you return to Africa and your husband then decides to abandon you and end your marriage, what would you do?" I was like "no he cannot leave me" I said so because our church had taught us that marriage was for better for worse, till death do us part. So, I never imagined that my husband would divorce me for any reason.

Some days later, I began to receive calls from different people asking me why I left my husband. He had given my phone number to different people and told them I left him. I got calls from England, Paris, and different places. They all asked the same questions when they called: "why did you leave your husband?" I told them I didn't leave my husband and that he approved of my trip before I travelled. Some offered to come to Paris to talk to me and advise me on what to do. I told them they shouldn't come and that they should ask my husband to call me. The only voice I needed so desperately to hear was my husband's. He still didn't call. My whole world was falling apart; I had been raped in my youth days, lost my business, abused and sex-starved in marriage by my husband, lost my dad, burdened by my sister's cancer diagnosis and I was about to lose my marriage. I asked myself: Why would life single me out to suffer so many troubles and pain?

While I was still trying to process all that was happening to me, a friend of mine by the name of Thelma called my sister and said she was in Paris and would love to meet with me. When we eventually met, she asked me why I left my husband and why I didn't want to return home. I told her my husband has refused to pick my calls and it was already five months since I arrived in France. I told her I almost ran mad because of the trauma of not hearing from my husband since I left Nigeria. I told her my pastor in Nigeria had earlier called and asked me to come back home but I refused because I needed to hear from my husband first. I explained everything to Thelma, and she saw reasons with me. Thelma went to Nigeria and spoke with him as she had promised. The following week, I called my husband, and he answered the call. When he answered, I broke down in tears and started crying. I said "so, you didn't receive my calls because I am your wife, you answered because of my friend, Thelma". His response was "what do you want, was that why you called me?" He was sounding very angry, we had a very serious argument and I told him out of anger that if the marriage was not working anymore, let's just end it. While we were talking, the call went off again and again and he would not call back. I called back four times, and the call went off each time. After the fourth time, my sister said I shouldn't call him back anymore and that we should wait for him to call. Can you believe that my husband never called back?

One week later, my husband called me and said he was ready to end the marriage as I had requested. He said we were going to have a divorce. I pleaded with him and told him that whatever I said was out of anger and that I didn't mean to end our marriage. He was adamant. He said his mind was made up and that we must have a divorce. Soon, he began the process of divorce and in 2018, we officially got divorced. It was like my whole world crumbled before me while I stood looking helplessly. I knew the travails of life almost destroyed me in Nigeria, but I never thought that my life in Paris would serve me more pains and that it would begin with a divorce. Why me? "What did I do wrong that ugly circumstances were bent on strangling the life out of me? "I asked myself.

I thought those were all the travails I would face in Paris; I didn't know that it was only the beginning of sorrows. I forgot to mention that I arrived Europe in 2013 and my sister died of cancer in 2015. After my sister's death, I was devasted and felt like I have had enough of all the travails life could bring my way. I wept bitterly and sorrow filled my heart. Just before I could finish mourning my sister's demise, her husband began to make trouble with me. He was a Cameroonian and the father of her children. He said to me "we are at war". I didn't understand why he said we were at war; so, I asked him what he meant by that and reminded him that he was my brother-in-law; how could we be at war? He replied and said that since my sister was already dead, we no longer had anything in common. I knew why he was angry and made that statement. He and my sister had separated before her demise. He cheated on my sister and when she found out about it, she was angry and asked him for a separation; meaning they no longer lived in the same house. Since my sister was dead, he had no one else to pour out his anger **to**, other than me. He said I do not have a right to my sister's children anymore and that I should go back to Nigeria. I was dumbfounded and shattered; "how could you say such a thing to me? I lost my marriage, my business, left the comfort of my home country, Nigeria, to France just because I wanted to help your family; how could you pay me with such wickedness?" I asked him. He continued to make trouble with me.

One day, after I returned from the school where I was learning French, I noticed that the doors to our house were locked by the government because I suspected that my sister's husband had reported me to the authorities that I was not the rightful owner of the house. That was how I was sent out of the house and became homeless. If God didn't come to my rescue, I would have fainted that period. "How did the young brilliant Lola who excelled in school, in business and in ministry as a youth become the Lola that was abused in marriage, lost her business, suffered a divorce, lost her father and sister, and is now homeless in a foreign land?" I asked myself with anguish.

As a homeless person, I roamed the streets of Paris for almost a year with no place to call my own. Wandering up and down the streets, I saw hell and it occurred to me that everything I had suffered in the past was nothing compared to the travails I would encounter on the streets of Paris. After healing from the rape experience, I had in Nigeria; I never thought I would experience such a thing in my life again. Unfortunately for me, I was raped again on the streets of Paris. I do not know what trauma could be worse than being held against your will and violated the second time in your life. When I could not make sense of all the unpalatable events happening to me on my life's journey, I concluded that, all the travails of my life were there to make me lose my faith and hope in God. They were there to make me forget about the purpose and calling of God on my life. I lost almost everything I had but I decided I would never lose my faith and hope in God. I was comforted by this song by the Brooklyn tabernacle choir;

I've lost some good friends along life's way
Some loved ones departed in Heaven to choir.
But thank God I didn't lose everything
I've lost faith in people who said they cared
In the time of my crisis, they were never there
But in my disappointment, in my season of pain
One thing never wavered, one thing never changed.
I never lost my hope
I never lost my joy
I never lost my faith
But most of all
I never lost my praise
My praise's still here
My praise's still here
I've let some blessings slip away.
And I lost my focus and went astray
But thank God I didn't lose everything

I lost possessions that were so dear
And I've lost some battles by walking in fear
But in the midst of my struggles, in my season of
pain
One thing never wavered
One thing never changed
It never changed
I never lost my hope.

Maybe you are going through difficulties and travails in your life, and you have lost friends, family, loved ones, your marriage, business, money and many other things and you are about giving up on life and on God, I want you to hold on a little while longer. God is going to come through for you. If you give up on life now, you will become a total loser, but if you hold on a little bit, the tides might just turn in your favor. Sometimes, the most difficult points of our life's journey are those closest to our destination. Many people give up and surrender at such points not knowing how close they are to their destiny. It is a known fact that the darkest part of the night is the closest to morning. Hold on, your morning will come. Those who give up when the storm is boisterous make nothing worthy out of their lives, but those who have enough courage and hope to sail against the tides eventually reach their glory-land and actualize their dreams, purpose and ambitions.

Nuggets

- Before I got married, I had an idea of what I thought an ideal marriage should be like; a loving, caring, forgiving and romantic relationship between two adults who are committed to each other for the rest of their lives and living in peace and harmony.

- It wasn't long after I got married that I realized that successful marriages need work, and that marriage comes with a handful of challenges and troubles.

- When I could not make sense of all the unpalatable events happening to me on my life's journey, I concluded that all the travails of my life are there to make me lose my faith and hope in God. They are there to make me forget about the purpose and calling of God upon my life.

- Life's travails might make me lose everything I have on my way to destiny, but I have decided I would never lose my faith and hope in God.

- Maybe you are going through difficulties and travails in your life, and you have lost friends, family, loved ones, your marriage, business, money and many other things and you are about giving up on life and on God, I want you to hold on a little while longer. God is going to come through for you!

- If you give up on life now, you will become a total loser, but if you hold on a little bit, the tides might just turn in your favor.

- Sometimes, the most difficult paths of our life's journey are those closest to our destination. Many people give up and surrender at such points not knowing how close they are to their destiny.

- It is a known fact that the darkest part of the night is the closest to morning. Hold on, your morning will come.

- Those who give up when the storm is boisterous make nothing worthy out of their lives, but those who have enough courage and hope to sail against the tides eventually reach their glory-land and actualize their dreams, purpose and ambitions.

Chapter Eight
FIGHT THE GOOD FIGHT OF FAITH

L ife is a battlefield and as strange as that may sound to a lot of people, it is unfortunately true. We are in a constant battle for survival; we are fighting sicknesses and diseases, we are fighting with poverty, we are fighting to have enough food to eat, we are fighting to stay healthy, to keep our loved ones safe, secure and alive; we are fighting to be alive, to keep our marriages and relationships from failing; we are fighting to keep our jobs, our political power, our academic career and anything else you can think of. Many people do not know they are in a battle because they are not holding swords, shields and armor and before they realize it, life has defeated them; they have lost their jobs, their loved ones, their marriages, their houses, their health and sometimes their very lives. How do we fight and overcome all the travails of life? This chapter explains what weapons we need to fight and win in the battles of life.

The Victory that Overcomes the World

In a world of pain, sorrows, and troubles, it is necessary to acquaint oneself with the knowledge required to fight and win. Had I not understood this earlier in my life, all the troubles I went through would have completely defeated me; I would have given up on life and on God. The travails of my life were enough to make me commit suicide and just end everything so that I could leave this world of troubles forever. None of us loves trials, troubles, and hard times and we prefer to run to a place of peace and quietness. The reality of life, however, is that sometimes, the troubles of life ambush us in such a way that we have nowhere to run to or even the time to do so. Hence, we must stand face-to-face with them and fight. It is either we surrender or let the troubles of life defeat us or we stand battle-ready to fight and overcome them. In the fight for life, we sustain injuries, and bruises, and are left with scars and if we do not quit and give up on life, those scars become a testament that we fought with the troubles of life and conquered them. When I realized that my life would never be completely free from troubles and pains, I decided that giving up was not an option; I would rather learn to fight and win than run and quit. I knew I had a great destiny ahead of me; a purpose, a calling, dreams, and ambitions that I must fulfill before I exit the earth. I would not let the travails of my youth and my life steal every good thing the future holds for me. So, I learned to fight. And as you would expect, every battle I won over the challenges of life made me stronger and better prepared for the next one. When life was pouring all its venom on me, I got to a point when it became clear to me that if I do not look for a way to survive, life would crush me completely. Having spent my teenage years in ministry with fervent prayers, the study of the word, singing and preaching, it was easy for me to draw strength from the word of God. I ran to the scriptures to find out what God's word says about overcoming the world and its many challenges. One bible verse that opened my eyes to the winning strategy over the challenges of life was:

For whatsoever is born of God overcometh the world: and this is the victory that overcometh the world, even our faith.
(1 John 5:4 KJV)

I pondered on this verse over and again until it illuminated my spirit. I began to understand that the greatest weapon to overcoming the challenges of life is our faith. Our world is full of troubles, trials, hard times and sorrows but there is one thing

*that overcomes the world and all its troubles; that is our faith.
Faith is therefore a defense, an armor of war. Without faith, no
battle can be won. It doesn't matter whether we are talking
about fighting sicknesses, diseases, death, marital challenges or
barrenness, without faith, you can never win. Faith is the
greatest force to overcoming the world! When I understood this, I
made up my mind that no matter what I lose on my life's
journey, I would never lose my faith. The man who loses faith in
life, has lost everything. He who loses faith in war, would soon
become a victim or spoil of war. It doesn't matter the size of the
obstacles and challenges on your way to destiny, with faith you
can overcome. It was thanks to faith that little David defeated
the giant Goliath in the bible. He believed that with God on his
side, Israel would win over the philistines and Goliath.
Without military armor, prior military training, David
through the power of faith, took a stone, put it in a sling and
defeated Goliath and won the victory for Israel in 1 Samuel 17.*

**45 Then said David to the Philistine, Thou
comest to me with a sword, and with a spear, and
with a shield: but I come to thee in the name of the
Lord of hosts, the God of the armies of Israel,
whom thou hast defied.**
**46 This day will the Lord deliver thee into mine
hand; and I will smite thee, and take thine head
from thee; and I will give the carcases of the host**

of the Philistines this day unto the fowls of the air, and to the wild beasts of the earth; that all the earth may know that there is a God in Israel.

47 And all this assembly shall know that the Lord saveth not with sword and spear: for the battle is the Lord's, and he will give you into our hands.

48 And it came to pass, when the Philistine arose, and came, and drew nigh to meet David, that David hastened, and ran toward the army to meet the Philistine. 49 And David put his hand in his bag, and took thence a stone, and slang it, and smote the Philistine in his forehead, that the stone sunk into his forehead; and he fell upon his face to the earth.

50 So David prevailed over the Philistine with a sling and with a stone, and smote the Philistine, and slew him; but there was no sword in the hand of David. 51 Therefore David ran, and stood upon the Philistine, and took his sword, and drew it out of the sheath thereof, and slew him, and cut off his head therewith. And when the Philistines saw their champion was dead, they fled. 52 And the men of Israel and of Judah arose, and shouted, and pursued the Philistines, until thou come to the valley, and to the gates of Ekron.

And the wounded of the Philistines fell down by the way to Shaaraim, even unto Gath, and unto Ekron.
(1 Samuel 17:45-52 KJV)

From the verse above, we see that David could speak with so much boldness even though he had no military weapons and training because he believed; he had faith that he would defeat Goliath and all the Philistine armies. When you have faith, it shows in your confessions. What you say in the face of your travails and troubles is proof of your faith or lack of faith. If you say you would be defeated and that you cannot win, that is exactly what would happen. If you say that this mountain is surmountable, it will give way before you know it. It is all about your faith. You win over the troubles of life thanks to your faith.

If you, therefore, must lose anything in your life and in battle, it must never be your faith. The reason the challenges of life are hitting you from every angle is that the enemy wants you to lose your faith and give up. The very moment you lose your faith, you have lost the battle and the challenges of life will overwhelm you. Therefore, you must guard your faith, for it is the greatest shield you have over the troubles of life. Your first fight in the battles of life

FIGHT THE GOOD FIGHT OF FAITH

should be a fight to protect your faith. It is a fight of faith. Faith is the victory that overcomes the world and all its troubles.

While it is true that you need faith to win over the challenges of life, I want you to know that you need more than just faith. You need armor that protects your whole being.

Put on Your Whole Armor

Historians say that Paul the Apostle was being guarded by Roman centurions while he was to be taken before Ceasar for trial. During that time, he wrote many books of the Bible through the inspiration of the Holy Spirit. He also used images of things around him to capture the essence of the ideas he was putting down in his books and letters. One of such instances is when he used a Roman Centurion's armor to describe the armor of God:

Put on the whole Armor of God, that ye may be able to stand against the wiles of the devil. For we wrestle not against flesh and blood, but against principalities, against powers, against the rulers of the darkness of this world, against spiritual wickedness in high places. Wherefore take unto you the whole Armor of God, that ye may be able to withstand in the evil day, and having done all, to stand. Stand therefore, having your loins girt about with truth, and having on the breastplate of righteousness.

And your feet shod with the preparation of the gospel of peace; Above all, taking the shield of faith, wherewith ye shall be able to quench all the fiery darts of the wicked. And take the helmet of salvation, and the sword of the Spirit, which is the word of God:18 Praying always with all prayer and supplication in the Spirit, and watching thereunto with all perseverance and supplication for all saints.
(Ephesians 6: 11-18 KJV)

From the verses above, we see that to fight and win the battles of life, we need to put on full armor. In the days of evil, the days of adversity and troubles, you will only be able to withstand the weapons fashioned against you if you put on complete armor. To stand strong and not faint in the days of adversity, you need more than just faith. You must add other weapons to your faith. Let's analyze the verses above and see what makes up a complete armor against the forces of evil that try to stop us from fulfilling our purpose and actualizing our dreams.

The first piece of armor we see is *"truth"*. The scripture says, *girt your loins with truth*. When you live a life of truth and stand always on the side of truth, you can be rest assured that you will win over the battles of life. Truth always wins in the end. So, no matter the forces and lies that are against you and trying to truncate your destiny, if you stay on the side of truth always, you will win in the end. For as Paul puts it in his letter to the Corinthians, nothing can be done against the truth, but for the truth. You must always learn to trust the truth of God's word about your situation. Do not live according to the realities of the circumstances that you are experiencing, live according to the realities of what God's word says about those circumstances. Do not confess the circumstance; confess the truth of God's word about it. That is why *the weak must say I am strong, and the poor must say I am rich*. God's word is truth and if God says anything about your situation that is the truth of the matter. Anybody who says otherwise is a liar.

-The second armor we see from the verses we read is **righteousness.** It says having on the breastplate of righteousness. When you live in righteousness, you easily overcome the troubles of life that come against you and whatever conspiracy that is being plotted against you fails eventually. It is almost impossible for the travails of life to completely defeat the man who is wearing *the breastplate of righteousness*. Living righteous doesn't mean you will not face the difficulties and troubles of life; you will, however, no matter how many troubles you face, you will prevail in the end. The Bible says that *the righteous man falls seven times and rises again*. So, yes, a righteous man can fall, but he will never stay down forever; he soon rises and walks victoriously to his glorious destiny.

The third piece of armor described in the passage is the **gospel of peace**; it says, and your feet shod with the preparation of the gospel of peace. The gospel is the goodnews, and the gospel of peace is the good news of peace. Always be on the side of peace and proclaim peace over your storms. "Peace, be still" should never depart from your lips. Speak it always to the circumstances of your life and they will obey. Rebuke the winds of troubles that try to rock your boat on your life's journey and calm would return.

The armor also consists of weapons and the fourth part you need to fight the battles of life is the **shield of faith;** it says: *and above all take the shield of faith, wherewith ye shall be able to quench all the fiery darts of the wicked*. Faith is a shield, and it doesn't just shield you from a few enemy arrows, it shields you from all their fiery darts.

The next weapons you need are the **helmet of salvation,** the sword of the spirit, which is the *word of God,* and *praying in the spirit* with *perseverance.*

When you are a believer, it means that you are saved and when the travails of life and the arrows of the enemy are thrown at you, the only sword that should be in your hand and on your lips is the word of God. The word of God is a spiritual sword and the man who fights with it, will surely win. That was the secret of David; while Goliath was throwing curses at David, David fought him with the word of God and won. You too must fight with the word of God. Proclaim always what God's word says about your situation. In the same vein, you must be a person of prayer. The battles of life cannot be won without prayers. Pray fervently, be instant in season and out of seasons. *The effectual fervent prayer of the righteous man always prevails.* Your prayer is your weapon of war. It first goes to God as a fragrance and then turns to fire to burn the obstacles that are standing on your way to destiny. You must persevere in the place of prayers and fight. The man who fights with the whole armor and the weapons is *fighting the good fight of faith* and would eventually win.

Fight the Good Fight of Faith with Lola

After I understood the secrets of winning over life's battles by putting on the whole armor of God, I began to see the troubles of life from a different perspective. I also began to realize that I actually have what it takes to fight and win. I resolved to no longer live with a victim's mentality or let the troubles of life stop me from fulfilling my God-given purpose. It was time to walk into that purpose that God had prepared me right from my teenage years. It is true that on my life's journey, I was raped twice, physically, and emotionally abused by my husband, lost my marriage, lost my business, lost my dad, lost my sister to cancer, became homeless and traumatized in Paris, but I refused to lose my faith or give up on life. I resolved to live on with determination and faith that the purpose of my being is actualizable. I decided to live my life to the fullest, taking every event of the past as preparation and training for the glorious destiny ahead of me. I felt a lot like Jonathan Anthony Burkett who in his book "Neglected", explained what it feels like to be attacked on every side without anyone to look up to for help but still have faith and conviction to hang in there with expectation:

"Feeling like, life has been so unfair to me, but what can I say except, "I'm still here." So, I'm determined to make the best out of it, take every opportunity as a blessing, and live the rest of my life to the fullest."

For me to heal and be able to fight, I needed to first fulfil the purpose for which I came to France; to take care of my sister's children. You would recall that their father had denied me access to them and rendered me homeless. One day while I was still roaming the streets of Paris, I got a call from my brother in-law and when I answered, he told me he was **moving** from Paris to Guiana and that he would take the children along. That meant I would no longer see the children again since they would be leaving Paris. Earlier on, my brother who was living in Spain had asked me to relocate to Spain, but I refused because I wanted to be in the same city with my sister's children. However, when their father moved them to Guiana, I had to call my brother and told him I was now ready to come to Spain. The following week, I landed in Spain.

In Spain, I was stressed and worn out from the trauma of losing my belongings and my accommodation in Paris and being homeless. It took me three years of taking medications in Spain to regain my strength and my sanity and to recover from the pain of three traumatic years of my life. I was introduced to a church in Spain, and I started attending, but later left that church for another church.

One day, my brother-in-law called me and told me that his children said they would love to go back to Paris but that he would not be going back with them. He said he would send the children to his brother in Paris. I said: "Ok!" His brother and my sister were sworn enemies while she was alive. Her enemy was now going to have custody of her children. I was very concerned about that, and I told him that after he sends the children to Paris, I would also leave Spain and return to Paris so that I could be close to the children. He said I would still not have access to them even if I return to Paris and I said that it was fine as long as I was on the same soil with them. So, I eventually returned to Paris after my brother in Spain relocated to the UK and I was once again in the same city with my sister's children.

One day in Paris, I got a call from my brother-in-law, and he told me that the government took his children from him. I later found out that his younger brother was maltreating them and physically abusing them under the guise that he wanted to discipline them. For almost two and a half years before this incident, I was in Paris, but this cruel man didn't allow me to see the children. I went through so much emotional trauma and would sometimes cry at night for not being allowed to see these children. It got to a point that one day I was almost running mad and just walking from one bus station to the other looking for these children. So, a man I had met in Spain called me; he was the President of Nigerians in Diaspora Organization (NIDO), Spain chapter and he goes by the name Chief Andrew Iduh. He asked what I was doing, and I told him about the stress I was going through and how it's almost driving me crazy. He told me not to hurt myself, that the children should be fine and living their lives. I told him that could be true but that I am worried about them and really need to see them.

The following Sunday, I went to my in-law's brother's house and demanded to see the kids. Unfortunately, the kids were not home as he had sent them somewhere to spend the day. He asked me to check back on another day. It was the day one of the kids would be having her birthday. I was so happy that I would eventually see my sister's children after almost four years of being apart. On that day, I arrived at his

OVERCOMING LIFE'S TRAVAILS

house as early as 8am and waited for the kids to get out of bed. When they came to the sitting room, they couldn't recognize me until they were told it was me. They were so excited and ran to me to hug me. They told me how much they missed me. We were so happy and had a good time before I left. From that time, I began to plead with him to grant me access once in a while to see the children. He agreed and that was how I started visiting the children once or twice a month. That was a very sweet experience for me because it healed me. At last, the purpose for which I left Nigeria for France was being realized.

On September 30th, 2018, I was looking up to God and asking Him to tell me about my life; what He would have me do? God spoke to me and said: "Lola, you are dimming my light!" I was shocked and didn't understand. So, I asked God "how am I dimming your light, Lord?" I eventually understood what God meant because I knew I was not fulfilling the purpose of my life, my ministry and calling at that time. I felt indicted and told God I was sorry and that He should forgive me. That night, I came downstairs and prayed throughout the night while I listened to the audio bible. I prayed until I had a shift in my spirit. I knew something had happened in the spirit realm; I had won a major battle and would break forth into a new phase of my life.

Then on the 1st of October, I was taking my bath when God spoke to me and said "I want you to go on social media and start *Fight the Good Fight of Faith with Lola Ministry*. I quickly answered in the affirmative because I knew I was born to impact lives and live for the extraordinary. It was time for me to *rise above life's travails and embrace the extraordinary within me.* I was born for this cause and I must live for this cause. Two weeks later, I travelled to Spain and continued to pray about this higher calling and ponder how I would go about it. Thankfully, we had a vigil in Spain, and I saw the cameraman that covered the vigil. The following day, I spoke with him and told him about what God had asked me to do on social media. I asked if he could help me. He agreed and on the 12th of October 2018, we shot the first episode of *Fight the Good Fight of Faith with Lola Ministry.*From that day, I would take a topic weekly and teach on it and post it on Facebook. As the ministry grew, we opened a group page on Facebook with the same name. We also wanted to impact beyond Facebook and decided to open a WhatsApp group.

However, I didn't know exactly how to go about it. As I stated in a previous chapter, I needed a mentor to guide me and show me the way. Thankfully for me, I had previously been introduced by a friend to a WhatsApp group called *'Developing Women to Survive Empowerment Initiative'(DWSEI).* While in the group, I met with the administrator, Mrs Abimbola Onwuchekwa and spoke to her about what God had asked me to do. I told her that what she was doing was exactly what God wanted me to do but that I didn't know how to go about it. She encouraged me and told me not to give up and that if God had asked me to do it, then I must do it. She took up the role of a mentor in my life from that day and made sure that I chose a specific date on which I would start my own WhatsApp group for my outreach *'Fight the Good Fight of Faith with Lola Ministry'.* She coached me and followed me up until the date I had chosen and made sure I opened the group on that day. It was the 21st of June 2020-my birthday. She continued to mentor me and correct my mistakes after I opened the group until I learned how to properly manage it.

We started small and gradually grew in numbers. We got to the point where we started inviting different resource persons to come and teach and impact members of the group. We have had over 24 different guest speakers impacting and teaching on different life-changing topics. So many testimonies have been shared by members of the group on how it has changed their lives. That group has become a huge success and a source of blessing to many people around the world. We have members from France, Spain, United States of America, United Kingdom, Kenya, Nigeria, Ghana, UAE, and many other countries across the world.

I feel so fulfilled and happy that I am at last living my purpose and impacting the world despite all the travails I had gone through. It is now clearer to me why I had to go through the path that I took. Those teenage years of fervency in the work of the kingdom, the travails and pain along the journey were all to prepare me and bring me to my promised land- my place of purpose, impact and fulfilled dreams. **Besides *Fight the Good Fight of Faith with Lola Ministry*, I am also blessing the world with my music ministry, and I have become an author.** Today, I am using my story to impact and inspire people across the world. The core of my message is no matter the troubles, pain and travails they would face on their life's journey, they must never faint and give up on life; but instead, fight the good fight of faith, believe in the beauty of their dreams and strive until they get to their promised land. You were created for a purpose and as you journey towards that purpose, you would meet obstacles, difficulties and suffer travails; don't quit, they are there to prepare you for a glorious destiny. Be strong, fight the good fight of faith, overcome the travails of your life, and enter into your promised land. If I could do it, you could do it too.

See you at the top!

Nuggets

- Life is a battlefield and as strange as that may sound to a lot of people, it is true. We are in a constant battle for survival; we are fighting sicknesses and diseases, we are fighting poverty, we are fighting to have enough food to eat, we are fighting to stay healthy, to keep our loved ones safe, secure and alive; we are fighting to be alive, to keep our marriages and relationships from failing; we are fighting to keep our jobs, our political power, our academic careers and anything else you can think of.

- None of us loves trials, troubles, and hard times. We prefer to run to a place of peace and quietness. The reality of life, however, is that sometimes, the troubles of life ambush us in such a way that we have nowhere to run to or even the time to do so. Hence, we have to stand face-to-face with them and fight.

- It is either we surrender and let the troubles of life defeat us or we stand battle-ready to fight and overcome them.

- In the fight for life, we sustain injuries, and bruises, and are left with scars and if we do not quit and give up on life, those scars become a testament that we fought with the troubles of life and conquered them.

- When I realized that my life would never be completely free from troubles and pains, I decided that giving up was not an option; I would rather learn to fight and win than run and quit.

- Faith is the greatest force to overcoming the world! When I understood this, I made up my mind that no matter what I lose on my life's journey, I would never lose my faith.

- The man who loses faith in life has lost everything. He who loses faith in war, would soon become a victim or spoil of war.

- It doesn't matter the size of the obstacles and challenges on your way to destiny, with faith you can overcome, without faith you will be overcome.

- If you must lose anything in your life and in

battle, it must never be your faith. The reason the challenges of life are hitting you from every angle is that the enemy wants you to lose your faith and give up.

• The very moment you lose your faith, you have lost the battle and the challenges of life will overwhelm you. Therefore, you must guard your faith, for it is the greatest shield you have from the troubles of life.

Reference

https://lifewithoutlimbs.org/about/nick-biography/
1.
https://www.learningliftoff.com/overcoming-obstacles-how-helen-keller-made-a-difference/
2.
https://www2.cbn.com/news/us/my-father-raped-me-least-200-times-joyce-meyer-says-shes-living-proof-recovery-sexual-abuse
3.
https://www.imdb.com/name/nm0583218/bio/
4.
https://praisehouston.com/3982381/pastor-paula-white-breaks-silence-on-divorce-stroke-and-her-alleged-affai/
5.
https://paulawhite.org/about/
6.
https://history.vcu.edu/news/newsroom/history-

news/humanity-equality-and-peace-the-life-and-vision-of-nelson-mandela.html

7.

https://www.thehistorymakers.org/biography/honorable-benjamin-carson-sr

8.

https://oc87recoverydiaries.org/get-help-for-depression-and-anxiety/

9.

Connect With Me on SOCIAL MEDIA

https://www.facebook.com/AjikeolaOmololah

https://www.instagram.com/lolageorge467/

https://www.instagram.com/FGFFWithLola/

https://www.youtube.com/@AJIKELOLA

https://www.tiktok.com/@fightoffaithwithlola

Made in the USA
Middletown, DE
27 October 2023